It is a privilege for me to recommend *Musical Discernment* for anyone who is looking for a common sense, practical, readable book on the relationship between music and morality.

It will help any reader develop a useful down-to-earth philosophy of how the written word and written music are connected, and how to share a Biblical approach with those who disagree with you. I look forward to adding this book to my library of helpful guidance and wisdom for Christians in their musical choices.

DR. FRANK GARLOCK
Founder of Majesty Music

Musical Discernment

Musical
Discernment

Elizabeth King

ISBN 978-1-7773093-0-5

All Scripture quotations are from the King James Version.

Proofreading by Sarah Wiens
Interior Design and Layout by J. Hodgins

Printed in Canada.
First printing September 2020

MusicalDiscernment@protonmail.com

Dedication

It is with deep pleasure that I welcome David into our family. As a recent addition to this clan, I pray that he may feel the love with which he is welcomed. Since David was a large part of the impetus of the writing of this book, I dedicate it to him as an explanation of part of the uniqueness of the upbringing of the woman he has chosen to marry.

I would also like to dedicate this book to Emily, a new daughter-in-law whom we have already grown to love. May this book explain to you the musical convictions of this family in general, and your new husband in particular.

Musical Discernment is also dedicated to Phoebe, soon to be a daughter-in-law. We've known you forever and loved you for almost as long. May this book be a blessing in the life of the family you're about to begin with our son.

Table of Contents

Introduction

Many times over the years, people have asked me to explain why I believe as I do about music. I have attempted to address each person at his or her level, and to communicate those things about music that I felt were the most applicable to his or her situation. However, the human mind is only able to take in a certain amount of new material at a sitting, and so in each encounter I have only brushed the surface of the philosophy of discernment in music. To some I have stressed the scientific evidences of the effects of music; others I have challenged to strive for excellence in godliness in all areas of their lives. I have challenged some people with the thought that we should not base all our decisions on our own fleshly desires. At length, when it became obvious that I would never be able to express everything in one sitting or even in a series of conversations, it was impressed upon me that I must write it all down.

It is important to me especially that my future daughters- and sons-in-law understand the importance of discernment in the realm of music. These people are taking my carefully nourished children as their spouses, and it is my desire that their homes become havens which show the love and the holiness of God. I want my grandchildren to be brought up in environments that provide all that they need for life and godliness. I yearn for them to be protected from those things which will be harmful to their minds, their souls, their relationships with others, and most importantly, their spirits.

I also wish to impart, to all those who wish to learn it, the basis for the belief that music communicates morality from the performer to the listener. This communication bypasses our minds to a great extent, so that mere exposure to music will begin to change us, and intentional listening crafts our souls into those which resemble the characters of the creators of the music. Our spirits are of such value to God that He sent His only begotten Son to provide eternal salvation to us, at an immense cost to Himself. Should we not, therefore, be faithful to safeguard our own souls and the souls of our children in every respect, as much as it is our responsibility to do so?

May this book be a blessing to all who read it. I think that it will anger some of you. To some it will be a curiosity. But I hope that to some of you, the truths of Scripture, of science, and of experience will reach into your spirits and call you to the excellence of following God in all areas of your lives—including in the area of music.

CHAPTER 1
The Beginning of Music

As we prepare to tackle the subject of morality in music, it makes sense to start at the beginning. No, even before the beginning. Before man arrived on the scene, before there was ever a debate as to music styles—back when God considered the elements of His creation—there was music.

When exactly did music begin? Music was created by God even before He created man. The Bible tells us that in the creation, the morning stars sang together. Were those morning stars, perhaps, the embodiment of the angels?

> Where wast thou when I laid the foundations of the earth? declare, if thou hast understanding. Who hath laid the measures thereof, if thou knowest? or who hath stretched the line upon it? Whereupon are the foundations thereof fastened? or who laid the corner stone thereof; When the morning stars sang together, and all the sons of God shouted for joy? (Job 38:4–7)

We see in the Scriptures that Satan was an important angel before the fall, and had pipes and tabrets with which he would have made music. He was, apparently, a skillful musician. Ezekiel 28 describes the king of Tyre:

> Moreover the word of the LORD came unto me, saying, Son of man, take up a lamentation upon the king of Tyrus, and say unto

him, Thus saith the Lord GOD; Thou sealest up the sum, full of wisdom, and perfect in beauty. Thou hast been in Eden the garden of God; every precious stone was thy covering, the sardius, topaz, and the diamond, the beryl, the onyx, and the jasper, the sapphire, the emerald, and the carbuncle, and gold: the workmanship of thy tabrets and of thy pipes was prepared in thee in the day that thou wast created. Thou art the anointed cherub that covereth; and I have set thee so: thou wast upon the holy mountain of God; thou hast walked up and down in the midst of the stones of fire. Thou wast perfect in thy ways from the day that thou wast created, till iniquity was found in thee... Thine heart was lifted up because of thy beauty, thou hast corrupted thy wisdom by reason of thy brightness: I will cast thee to the ground, I will lay thee before kings, that they may behold thee. (Ezekiel 28:11–17)

Although this passage is addressed to the king of Tyre, it is apparent that it also applies to a spiritual being who was in the garden of Eden, is called a cherub, and was upon the holy mountain of God. Don Stewart and other theologians conclude that while the passage did apply to the actual king of Tyre, it in a deeper sense is addressed to Satan.[1] If indeed this passage speaks of Satan, we see that he is described as being beautiful and perfect in the beginning of his creation. His adorning jewels are mentioned, as well as the tabrets and pipes which presumably were indicative of his abilities in music. When Satan fell, he was cast out of heaven with the rest of the angels that sinned. Where did he go? This passage indicates that he was present in the garden of Eden. He is the one who enticed Eve to commit the original sin—the defying of God's authority in eating the fruit of the one tree that was forbidden to the first humans God created. Since then, Scripture tells us in Job that he's been wandering about the whole earth.

Now there was a day when the sons of God came to present themselves before the LORD, and Satan came also among them. And the LORD said unto Satan, Whence comest thou? Then Satan answered the LORD, and said, From going to and fro in the earth, and from walking up and down in it. (Job 1:6–7)

Satan's business is to sow doubt and discouragement, defilement and death, among believers and unbelievers alike. He is sly and subtle in the way he goes about this subversive work. When he appears to people to tempt them to sin, he doesn't show himself as an ugly, scary red creature with a pitchfork in his hand. No, he appears as an angel of light.

> For such are false apostles, deceitful workers, transforming themselves into the apostles of Christ. And no marvel; for Satan himself is transformed into an angel of light. Therefore it is no great thing if his ministers also be transformed as the ministers of righteousness; whose end shall be according to their works. (II Corinthians 11:13–15)

Satan and his evil workers tempt us with things that are appealing to us. To Eve, it was the one fruit she had been forbidden to eat that was her downfall; for politicians, it may be the hope of power and prominence; for young men, the pleasure of sexual sin sometimes proves to be their undoing. Could it be that Satan uses his prowess at music to deceive and seduce people into sins of the flesh? Jesus said that His sheep hear His voice, and follow Him. But sometimes I fear that the musical devil can attract our ear so that we may think we're following the voice of the Shepherd when we're actually following the voice of the devil.

We don't know that much about the garden of Eden. How long were God's first humans there? What did they talk about? Did Adam and Eve sing in the garden? Who knows but that the original language of mankind was music? Perhaps every word they spoke was a song. I'm not suggesting this as doctrine, but because music is so integral to the human soul, I do wonder about the way in which Adam and Eve communicated before the introduction of sin into the world.

Many centuries after Eden, Moses led the children of Israel out of slavery in Egypt. When they crossed the Red Sea and experienced freedom from their overlords for the first time in their lives, Moses taught them a song of victory and freedom:

> Then sang Moses and the children of Israel this song unto the Lord, and spake, saying, I will sing unto the Lord, for he hath triumphed

gloriously: the horse and his rider hath he thrown into the sea. The Lord is my strength and song, and he is become my salvation: he is my God, and I will prepare him an habitation: my father's God, and I will exalt him. (Exodus 15:1–2)

The song carries on through several more verses, exultantly expressing the people's joy at the deliverance provided for them by God. And yet, just weeks later, these same Israelites get tired of waiting for Moses to come down from the mountain where God has been giving him the Ten Commandments. They make a golden calf, and as Moses and Joshua descend the mountain, Moses describes the sound that the worshippers of this golden calf make as singing. "And he said, It is not the voice of them that shout for mastery, neither is it the voice of them that cry for being overcome: but the noise of them that sing do I hear." (Exodus 32:18) In the case of the early Israelites, music was used to glorify God, and then to worship idols, with only weeks separating the two events.

Job described evil men who prosper as also enjoying music.

Wherefore do the wicked live, become old, yea, are mighty in power? … They take the timbrel and harp, and rejoice at the sound of the organ… Therefore they say unto God, Depart from us; for we desire not the knowledge of thy ways. (Job 21:7–14)

This passage describes those who prosper in life, having their needs met and enjoying leisure, including the performance of music. And yet, though every need has been supplied, they reject the knowledge of God. Doesn't that sound a lot like our current culture? All around us are people who thrive in an environment of culinary extravagance, educational advances, technological marvels, and excesses of entertainment, including the availability of all types of music. The response of so many, living in such a rich world, is to deny the very God who made it and them.

When the angels announced the Saviour's birth, was it with a song, as the carols say? Or is it just that the speech of angels, being uttered by beings straight from heaven, can't help but sound like magnificent singing? The singing of the angels is mentioned so often in carols that one has to wonder exactly what angels sound like when they speak, especially when we remember that the Bible often mentions the presence of music in heaven.

We do know that human beings have had music as part of their beings and their cultures for a very long time—archaeology indicates that we've had music since the beginning of life on earth. Stone flutes and ancient drums bear witness of mankind's long association with music. References to musical instruments in ancient cultures are common, both in the Bible and in secular accounts of history. King David, who lived a thousand years before Christ, was called the sweet psalmist of Israel. We have a record of the words of his songs in the Psalms. We know that he played the harp for King Saul, and it seems that he practiced that instrument during the long, solitary days and nights he spent watching his father's sheep. It was this skillful harpist who was called to come and play the music which would free Saul from tormenting spirits.

> And Saul's servants said unto him, Behold now, an evil spirit from God troubleth thee. Let our lord now command thy servants, which are before thee, to seek out a man, who is a cunning player on an harp: and it shall come to pass, when the evil spirit from God is upon thee, that he shall play with his hand, and thou shalt be well. And Saul said unto his servants, Provide me now a man that can play well, and bring him to me. Then answered one of the servants, and said, Behold, I have seen a son of Jesse the Bethlehemite, that is cunning in playing, and a mighty valiant man, and a man of war, and prudent in matters, and a comely person, and the LORD is with him. Wherefore Saul sent messengers unto Jesse, and said, Send me David thy son, which is with the sheep. And Jesse took an ass laden with bread, and a bottle of wine, and a kid, and sent them by David his son unto Saul. And David came to Saul, and stood before him: and he loved him greatly; and he became his armourbearer. And Saul sent to Jesse, saying, Let David, I pray thee, stand before me; for he hath found favour in my sight. And it came to pass, when the evil spirit from God was upon Saul, that David took an harp, and played with his hand: so Saul was refreshed, and was well, and the evil spirit departed from him. (I Samuel 16:15–23)

It's interesting to note here that when David played his harp, the evil spirit which had been troubling Saul departed from him. English theologian F. D. Maurice believed that

> The music was more than a mere palliative. It brought back for the time the sense of a true order, a secret, inward harmony, an assurance that it is near every man, and that he may enter into it[2].

When one investigates what this "evil spirit" could be, one finds that many Christian theologians do believe that it was an actual spiritual being who was bothering King Saul. Interestingly enough, the record of this evil spirit disturbing the king comes after the account of Saul's rebellion which caused him to eventually lose the kingship of Israel. It is no coincidence that an evil spirit is associated with one who is rebellious: we see in I Samuel 15:23 that "rebellion is as the sin of witchcraft."

We don't know whether David sang while he played for Saul, though it is likely, considering the many Psalms he authored. Whether the music had lyrics or not, we know that it had a spiritual impact on the listener: it was used to remove an evil spirit from Saul. If we are to take the Bible literally, we need to recognize that music does have a very real spiritual impact on those who listen to it. And if it can have a positive spiritual impact, as it did when David played for Saul, it is logical to conclude that some music can also have a negative spiritual impact.

Through the Psalms, we are told frequently to sing to God. It's given as a command, because singing is an important part of worship which is near to the heart of God. However, music continues to be used as an element of pagan worship too.

Later in life, David became the king of Israel. His son Solomon built the Temple, and the dedication of the Temple was celebrated with trumpeters, singers, cymbals, and other instruments of music. In consideration of these two great, musical kings of Israel, J. S. Bach wrote in his Bible, "A splendid example, that … music … was especially ordered by God's spirit"[3] and "With devotional music, God with His grace is always present."[4]

The book of Daniel gives the account of three friends who refused to cooperate when music called them to worship idols.

> . . . at what time ye hear the sound of the cornet, flute, harp, sackbut, psaltery, dulcimer, and all kinds of musick, ye fall down and worship the golden image that Nebuchadnezzar the king hath set up. (Daniel 3:5)

Daniel's three friends were thrown into the fiery furnace simply because they did not respond to the music in the required way, which was to fall down and worship the idol. As we know, God delivered them from dying that fiery death.

Music is mentioned several times in the New Testament, too. In Ephesians 5:19, Paul tells Christians to be "Speaking to yourselves in psalms and hymns and spiritual songs, singing and making melody in your heart to the Lord." It's interesting to see that there is a distinction here between types of acceptable Christian music. Psalms are those songs written down in God's songbook, the book of Psalms. These lyrics have been used for millennia when God's people have come before Him. The psalms were used by the early church, and even today, some denominations believe that settings of the Psalms are the only music that should be used in corporate worship.

Hymns are songs which are written for congregational singing. They normally have a reasonably simple melody, and are often arranged in four-part harmony. For the most part, hymns tend to focus on God and His attributes, and the doctrines presented in hymns are often taken right out of Scripture.

Spiritual songs can be less formulaic in structure than hymns, but are still distinguishable from secular forms of music by the word "spiritual." This would definitely refer to the words of the song: they must be on a spiritual theme. But could the word spiritual also refer to the music itself?

The power of good music over the soul of man has been affirmed throughout history. Shu Ching, in the 6th century BC, wrote, "For changing people's manners and altering their customs there is nothing better than music."[5] A little later Cassiodorus wrote,

> Music doth extenuate fears, furies, appeaseth cruelty, abateth heaviness and to such as are wakeful it causeth quiet rest; it cures all irksomeness and heaviness of the soul.[6]

In the first century before Christ, in ancient Greece, "Pythagoras quieted the perturbations of the mind with a harp."[7] From ancient times till today, music has had a powerful impact on the human soul.

CHAPTER 2

The Significance of Music

Music is ethereal; a matter of the spirit more than simply a concrete matter of notes, duration, and tempo. Who really invented it, after all? And what is it for?

Music is not essential to human communication. Birds sing—they broadcast with their songs that they are interested in a mate, or that it's morning, or just for the joy of it. But birds don't speak. Birdsong is their only audible means of communication.

Whales sing. Singing is also, for them, a means of communication. By it they locate their pods, identify themselves, and share thoughts. But they have no words. As far as human scientists have been able to determine, no wild animal actually has a vocabulary or uses words of any kind as a means of communication with another animal. Yes, apes can learn a limited vocabulary of human words. Dogs and cats can learn to recognize words and obey human commands. Although wild animals communicate through song, scent, body language, and sound, they never develop words, syntax, or formal language. But there's something different about humans. With words we give directions, teach concepts, encourage and discourage each other. We pen books and give lectures. We write blogs and jot grocery lists. We can communicate almost anything with the written word.

Then why do we sing? Ability in music does not guarantee one a long life, nor does it increase the likelihood of progeny. It does not automatically increase the pay grade of anyone but the most popular professional musicians. Music must be something that affects, not our physical life in this world primarily, but our souls, our spirits—the eternal, God-like parts of us. Music is universal. John Blacking, in his 1973 book *How Musical Is Man?* said that music transcends culture and time.

What does music do? The music that is added to lyrics intensifies emotion: making sharper or more poignant the pain, portraying the sunset more beautifully, deepening the joy. Music touches our souls in a way that words alone never can. As Oliver Sacks puts it, of all the arts, music "is the most closely tied to the emotions …"[1] It has a "peculiarly direct connection to the emotions."[2] Musicians find that, in order to perform a song well, they need to try to recapture the emotions they felt when they first wrote the song or lived the experiences that brought it about.

As human beings, music is of daily importance to us. We sing as we're washing the dishes, driving the car, or putting our baby to sleep. We listen to music on the radio, CDs, or our phones or computers while at home, in transit, or while shopping. We listen to music or are involved in it congregationally while at church, at a wedding, a funeral, or a sporting event. We spend money on better speakers for our cars, concert tickets, MP3s, music lessons and musical instruments. "Americans spend more on music than they do on prescription drugs."[3]

There exists plenty of music that does not, and never has, had words. Instrumental music can touch the soul just as well as music with lyrics can. Even without words, we recognize a sad song when we hear one. Joyful music can lift our spirits without the help of lyrics. People have tried to quantify the techniques whereby music is made to be sad or happy. Music that contains a preponderance of downward runs tends to make us sad, while music with upward skips tends to encourage happiness. Fast music tends to convey joy and energy, whereas slow music tends to melancholy and thoughtfulness. While these clues help us in a measure to understand the techniques of how to make music express the feelings we desire to communicate to others, there's something more. It's as if the composer puts something of his soul into the music; or at least, that music has the power to bypass our consciousness and directly touch our spirits.

The Rev. C. Kingsley wrote,

> There is something very wonderful in music. Words are wonderful enough: but music is even more wonderful. It speaks not to our thoughts as words do; it speaks straight to our hearts and spirits, to the very core and root of our souls. Music soothes us, stirs us up; it puts noble feelings into us; it melts us to tears, we know not how; it is a language by itself, just as perfect in its way as speech, as words; just as divine, just as blessed.

> Music has been called the speech of angels; I will go further, and call it the speech of God Himself … Yes, I say it with all reverence; but I do say it. There is music in God. Not the music of voice or sound; a music which no ears can hear, but only the spirit of a man, when awakened by the Holy Spirit, and taught to know God—Father, Son, and Holy Ghost… remembering, too, that music, like marriage, and all other beautiful things which God has given to man, is not to be taken in hand unadvisedly, lightly, or wantonly, but … reverently, discreetly, advisedly, soberly, and in the fear of God.[4]

So, why do we sing? Why do we play instruments? Is it the image of God inside us—in our very souls—which cries out for expression? Words alone can never be enough to contain the soul of man.

God commands us in Scripture to sing praises to Him, to make a joyful noise, and to sing a new song. Jesus and the disciples sang a hymn after the Last Supper. Music expresses worship and praise in a way that connects us to the heart of God like nothing else.

But beyond the usefulness of music in worship, I believe we have music because it can be beautiful, and our God is a God of beauty.

> The arts are not extraneous or a luxury in life, but they are a vital and essential part of our existence… Art comes from our being made in the image of God, and we know God is for the arts and has relegated to men and women wonderful gifts of creativity…

(W)e can delight in great paintings, architecture, literature, music, and so on, remembering that the living God gives us richly all things to enjoy (I Tim. 6:17). We do need to ask for discernment, though, so we will seek that which is wholesome and beautiful.[5]

CHAPTER 3
Early Written Music

Music has been part of the history of mankind as long as mankind has existed. Most music in the first five millennia of the world was learned by heart, as written music had not yet been developed. Isadore of Seville, in the seventh century, said, Unless sounds are held by the memory of man, they perish, because they cannot be written down.[1] The monks of ancient monasteries sang through the entire book of Psalms. Learning the tune to every psalm would require a phenomenal memory. Therefore, the monks began to develop a method of writing music down so that it could be read and performed reliably. One of our earliest examples of written music is a cuneiform tablet from Iraq, which gave fragmented instructions about the performance of the music written thereon. Ancient music showed symbols above words to indicate the melody. Gradually, written symbols for music developed: a series of squares was placed at varying heights relative to a central line. Over the centuries, attempts to show pitch gradually attained another line, and then another, until in about 1000 AD Guido d'Arezzo proposed the adoption of the four-line staff. Five-line staves showed up in Italy in the thirteenth century, but weren't standardized until around 1600. In terms of the actual notes written on those staff lines, by 850 AD, early musical notation had developed which bears some resemblance to today's notes.

Long after musical notation began to show tonality with any degree of reliability, there was no technique in place by which to show rhythm. It wasn't until the thirteenth century that notes showing different lengths began to be worked out. For instance, a note which was held for two beats was shown as a circle with a stem. Measures, which group notes into combinations totalling a determined number of beats, appeared in the 17th century.

Meanwhile, different cultures all around the world have used different patterns, or groupings, of notes to make music. Parts of the world have used a five-note, or pentatonic, scale as the basis for much of their music: for example, traditional Chinese music is pentatonic and sounds quite different from Western music. Throughout Europe in ancient times, there were eight modes used to compose music. Each mode was said to have a certain feel to it. Slowly the modes were replaced by the major and minor keys. Our Western system of having twelve major keys and twelve minor keys from which to choose was refined and formalized by Johann Sebastien Bach when he wrote his Well-Tempered Clavier in 1722. Major keys tend to lend themselves to upbeat, happier songs, while minor keys are often used to express sadness, mystery, or danger.

The entire world was created with scientific principles that support the playing of harmony-rich, beautiful music. When one taps a tuning fork, a note is produced. If there are other objects in the near environment which can ring to that same note, they will. Any note played on a piano will cause other strings to ring. Dampen the string that was played, and there will be other strings still vibrating, contributing to the full sound of music produced by the piano. The quiet sounding of each of these overtones gives the full richness we are accustomed to hearing in musical instruments.

God designed our brains to be in tune with the world He created. The physics of the world make it possible for overtones to be created, and our reliance on these overtones for the creation of musical scales and songs is no coincidence—it is just how God designed us. Even infants prefer what we would call consonance in music rather than dissonance.[2]

Written music is like written language—it codifies what is already being heard. And yet, written music represents played music better than written language represents spoken language. Our written language has generally been more formal than our spoken language. When we speak, we don't break up our thoughts into properly punctuated sentences; rather, we ramble on and mix our thoughts together, using casual language, and we tend to be careless about using proper grammar. Formal written language, on the other hand, must be properly spelled, punctuated, and indented; and must have proper grammar with well-formed sentences, not to mention a more precise vocabulary. Recently, when I transcribed a long meeting into written form, I avoided transcribing repetitions, um's, and interruptions. I tried to write every word that had any import. And so we see that written language is not a faithful reproduction of oral language.

Written music, however, is meant to be a very accurate indication of how the composer wants the played music to sound. Every note must be the exact length indicated by the music, and it must be the correct pitch, as well as the proper volume, or dynamic. Although a skilled soloist can introduce interpretation, variations, and improvisations, usually the music written for an orchestral concert or a first grade piano book is meant to be played exactly as written. Even during improvisation, the concepts of key (which combination of notes are played) and meter (the pattern of stressed beats) must be adhered to.

As we consider the history of the development of musical notation, it becomes obvious that we are quite unaware of how early music sounded. The modes, rhythms, meters and harmonies used in ancient music are, quite frankly, a mystery to us. But as musical notation became common, and as man became more literate, music began to develop in such a way that we can now look back and see its gradual transformation. From as far back as Medieval times, we can trace with some certainly the development of Western music and its uses.

Johann Gutenberg set his newly invented printing press into action in the mid-1400's, and shortly thereafter began the time period known as the Renaissance. This French word means "rebirth," because it was as if humanity had been reborn in mind and in spirit. The printing press allowed for a sharing of ideas which was to create immense sociological, scientific, and artistic developments throughout Europe and the world. Emblematic of the times in which Gutenberg lived, the Bible was the obvious choice to be the first book ever printed in this manner. Suddenly the Bible became available to upper class individuals, whereas previously it had been owned almost exclusively by the Church. Those who were educated enough to be able to read well and rich enough to own a Bible could now read it, discuss its concepts with others, and understand theology and other subjects in a deeper way than would have been possible previously.

God was working in the hearts of various men who were led to an understanding of salvation in Christ through the Scriptures. One of these, a German monk named Martin Luther (1483–1546), found that the truths contained in the Bible did not match the teachings of the Catholic church. In 1517, he hung up his 95 Theses on the door of the church he led in Wittenberg. This and other events led to the Reformation. Luther translated the Bible into German at the peril of his own life, so that the common people could read it for themselves. The truth published by Luther, Calvin and other preachers spread throughout Europe. The Bible, which had been chained to pulpits and forbidden from being translated into the language of the common people, was now not only translated, but printed in presses, making it affordable to the emerging middle class. Finally, congregations could hear the Word of God spoken in their language by their ministers, and the truths of Scripture were eagerly soaked up by many spiritually thirsty individuals. As biblical knowledge spread, a radical transformation in society occurred which brought God and truth to the foreground. Great strides began to be made in the sciences, literature, and the arts as a result.

Once the usefulness of the printing press became apparent, it was used to produce other books. Musicians, who for centuries had been labouriously copying out their musical works by hand, now had access to the printing press. This exciting development allowed music to travel beyond its country of origin and be available to a far broader audience. No individual composer could have had a large or lasting impact before the invention of the printing press.

The printing press allowed people to record the happenings of their daily lives. We find from early printed documents that it was common in Medieval times for doctors to call in minstrels to aid in the recovery of their patients, and that expectant mothers listened to music in the hope of increasing the well-being of themselves and their unborn children. Dentists employed musicians to play loudly while they operated on their patients. This may have distracted people from their pain, and masked the screams of the unsedated patients.

The monk Martin Luther was also a musician, and he wished to use music for God's glory. His belief in the power of music to elicit worship and give glory to God was so strong that he believed music to be second only to doctrine in the church. "Music is a gift of God, not a gift of men … After theology I accord to music the highest place and greatest honor."[3] He also declared, "I feel strongly that all the arts, and particularly music, should be used in the service of Him who has created and given them."[4] Luther wrote many hymns and encouraged congregational singing, "so that the Word of God may be kept alive in their hearts by song."[5] Luther wrote, "Beautiful music is the art of the prophets that can calm the agitations of the soul; it is one of the most magnificent and delightful presents God has given us."[6]. In these quotes Luther is referring to the preponderance of music that was available to him and in use in churches at the time: lovely songs, which followed the structures of orderly music meant to showcase beauty and to elicit worship from the hearts of mankind.

However, there was other music, even in Luther's time. In the preface of a hymn book Luther was involved in writing, he said, "I should like young people … to have at their disposal something which will rid their minds of lascivious and sensual songs, and teach them instead something wholesome." In this we see that there were forms of sensual music long before the introduction of rock or jazz. Luther believed that music could be used to edify believers, but he also knew that sensual music could corrupt people.

Whatever music was like at the beginning of time, the development of written music shows us that by the Baroque period, the concepts of modality, meter, and notation were firmly entrenched in works of intricate melody and harmony which we may still enjoy today. The Reformation, epitomized by Luther, created a spiritual climate which was ready to produce the most God-directed music in the history of mankind.

CHAPTER 4
Music History from the Baroque Era to the Present

Into the newly reformed Germany was born a musician whose genius is still revered by musicians the world over. Johann Sebastian Bach was part of a Christian family of musicians, and he produced an enormous quantity of music, most of which was written with the express purpose of glorifying God. Bach wrote,

> ... the end and ultimate cause ... of all music ... should be none else but the glory of God and the recreation of the soul/mind. Where this is not observed, there is no real music but only a devilish blare and hubbub.[1]

This resounds strongly with the Westminster Shorter Catechism, where it is declared that "The chief end of man is to glorify God and to enjoy Him forever." The period of time in which Bach lived is now called the Baroque era. Much of the music composed in Baroque times was composed for use in church. There were also operas and other forms of music, but this was a time when church and Christian living were together a strong driving force of the culture, and thus of the music of the era. The oratorio, a musical drama based on Biblical themes, became a more standardized form of music during this time.

Bach, a prodigious musician, held various musical positions. At this time, a musician could earn a living by being employed by a political leader or by a church; Bach spent time in both types of positions. His goal in religious compositions was to create "a well-ordered church music", which meant specific musical pieces for each feast day in the Lutheran church, as well as a full musical schedule for each Sunday in the year.

Bach produced musical sons who were also composers. When asked why his sons, more than most other Bach pupils, excelled in their music, he answered,

> Because they had, from their earliest youth, opportunity in their father's house to hear good music, and no other. They were therefore accustomed early, and even before they had received any instruction, to what was most excellent in the art.

Even during the Baroque era, there was music of good and bad moral quality. When Bach and his son Friedeman attended the opera, Bach called such musical offerings "ditties." He considered this music harmless and enjoyable. However, we can see that he did differentiate between godly music and ungodly music. He declared that when music was not composed for the glory of God and the enjoyment of man, what resulted was devilish hubbub. I often wonder what he would think of much of the music in the world today—including that within the church.

Music is a reflection of the culture around it. For instance, tribes deep in Africa, untouched by modern civilization until recent centuries, used music to worship their heathen deities. Surviving music from medieval times shows the preponderance of troubadours, the travelling musicians of the time. Romantic love was an important subject in their songs. Today's popular music dwells on the same subjects that the troubadours used, and also reflects other elements of our culture, such as the sexual revolution and race wars.

Music at the time of Bach also reflected his culture. Bach grew up in the same region of Germany as Luther had, and the explosion of biblical knowledge that had been ignited by the printing press and the Reformation was still glowing throughout that country. Biblical Christianity was the dominant religion, as Germany became a place of culture and refinement.

The music of Europe at that time was focussed on beauty, harmony, and balance. Intricate melodies interwove themselves through many layers of music, creating rich harmonies, tensions and resolutions. Rhythms were varied and complex, and yet stayed within the norm of stressing the first beat in each measure. In a piece of music in 4/4 time, beats one and three of each measure usually had new notes occurring on them, keeping the rhythmic balance of the piece on firm footing. The size of the orchestra was typically small: from fifteen to fifty players. Bach was a master of the technique of counterpoint; that is, he would write a piece of music that featured two, three or more melodies, all happening at the same time, and providing harmony through the way in which the melodies interacted.

Bach lived at the same time as Isaac Newton. The study of the sciences and the arts were far more intertwined during their time than in ours. Scientists and mathematicians observed the stars and invented mathematical theorem based on a knowledge of the Scriptures. They believed that the stars, the planets, the rules of math, and the rules of music and art all had balance and harmony. Scientists of the time believed that they could prove the characteristics of God by the orderly scientific principles they discovered. They believed that the harmony of all created things was implanted in them by our Divine Creator. A perfect 3-note chord represented the Holy Trinity to them. One particular 3-note chord was the C major triad; this chord was the beginning of the logic that inspired the development of Bach's *Well-Tempered Clavier*, the work that defined the 24 musical keys.[2]

> Bach chose to draw on the Scriptures, the well of life, for his inspiration and creativity, and he affirmed repeatedly that he wrote his music to the glory of God and with the help of Jesus. Most critics agree that Bach was the greatest composer of all time. A contemporary of Bach, Andreas Werckmeister, spoke of music as as gift of God to be used only in His honor... With his profound Christian understanding, Bach has had an enduring influence in music history in terms of health, strength, and order.[3]

Good things don't tend to last for very long, here on earth. Gradually, Christianity in Europe became more cultural than personal, and the religious fervour that had caused men to lose their lives for the sake of the gospel, when necessary, dimmed. Church became a place to attend for society's sake, and the lifestyles of many strayed from the purity of God's standards. The religious conservatism of the Baroque period gave way to the looser lifestyles of the Enlightenment. The hallmarks of this age were scientific reason, liberty for all, and tolerance. People began to more commonly reject the Church and the Bible as their authorities in life. Instead of relying on biblical teaching, they reasoned out their lifestyle choices based on what they chose to believe to be right. As the Bible says, Every man did that which was right in his own eyes. (Proverbs 21:2)

> Less than one hundred years after Bach, as the influence of the Enlightenment with its rejection of biblical Christianity began to be felt, Dr. Charles Burney in his General History of Music, wrote that music is an innocent luxury, unnecessary indeed to our existence, but a great improvement and gratification of the sense of hearing.[4]

Bach died in 1750. Dr. Burney wrote the above words in 1789. In four decades, music had gone from being used to the glory of God, to being an "innocent luxury", with no mention of God.

Music reflected the cultural shift of society. Many professional musicians of this age were not believers. They wrote songs, symphonies, cantatas and other forms of music for the enjoyment of the people. We call the musical period that happened after the Baroque the Classic Period. The musicians of this time included Mozart, Beethoven, and Haydn. Standing on the shoulders of their Baroque predecessors, they wrote music that was indeed beautiful. Still orderly, it left intricate counterpoint behind as the overdone relic of another age. Harmonies and keys were stretched to create tension and drama in music. While much of the music of the Baroque focussed on God, the music of the Classic period focussed on man and nature. For example, Beethoven's third symphony, The Eroica, was about his hero, Napoleon; the subject of his sixth symphony, the Pastoral Symphony, was nature. In the Classical era musicians began to make money by selling tickets to their concerts, rather than by producing music for an employer. Much of the music was truly lovely, and yet the spiritual dimension was lacking. In a culture which was moving away from godliness, the beauty of the music seemed to be enough—the general public apparently didn't miss the call of music to turn their hearts toward God.

The next musical period, which began around 1820, was the Romantic Period. The nineteenth century included such musicians as Rachmaninoff, Schubert and Liszt. Culturally, the thoughts of man turned more and more inward, and music reflected the grotesqueness of the thoughts of a man fully consumed with himself. Liszt performed so dramatically and violently that he regularly broke pianos apart on stage. In the Romantic Period, there developed the beginning of a "fan" mentality, where women would scream when Liszt came on stage, in a similar fashion to what happened when the Beatles performed a century later. While still maintaining the basic rules of rhythm and harmony, Romantic music displayed much drama, contrast, and unrest. Music written in minor keys flourished, and rhythms became more complex, and used a technique called rubato, where regular time was not strictly adhered to. No longer was music the portrayal of the beauty of God's order. Romantic music sought to stretch the sensibilities of its listeners, just as citizens of the western world were straining against the restrictions of a godly lifestyle.

The great Baroque composers Vivaldi, Bach, and Handel were devoted believers who produced extraordinary music. During the time that Handel was composing his oratorio *The Messiah*, he cried out, "I did think I did see all heaven before me, and the great God Himself!" Many have believed that Handel must have been inspired in order to be able to write such beautiful music in only a few weeks' time. In the Baroque period, shortly after the Reformation, Western European society was so thoroughly influenced by Christianity that much of the *secular* work these musicians composed had Christian references in the lyrics and was very like church music in style. In fact, many pieces of music were adjusted only slightly as they were borrowed from secular works to be utilized as church music or vice versa. But as society shifted from its spiritual foundation, music also changed. In the Classical period there were fewer professional Christian composers writing much less Christian music. By the time of the Romantic period, there were very few

Christian composers, and most music was not only written for secular purposes, but it was written without the harmony and balance that were typical of earlier music. Several Romantic composers were heavily involved in the occult, with a fascination for things that were morbid. Richard Wagner was the epitome of the anti-God sentiment common in music from the Romantic period. As society changed, the music changed, and now we can look back to see a range of music throughout the ages: both that which is beautiful and orderly, and that which is off-balance and disharmonic.

As the world entered the twentieth century, concert music began to diverge into two different tracks. Firstly, great musicians began taking themes from folk music and developing them into symphonic works. Composers such as Ralph Vaughn Williams and Bela Bartok utilized folk music in their compositions. Folk music tends to consist of short melodic segments of 4 or 8 bars in length, set to simple rhythms, with musical melodies. This is the music of the common folk—not the rich nor the intellectuals, who were the people who paid to attend concerts in this period. Vaughn Williams and Bartok incorporated folk music into their orchestral arrangements in such a way that it appealed to both the aristocrat and the peasant. Folk music was involved in everyday life at the turn of the century. Mothers sang lullabies to their babies, citizens sang national anthems, children sang songs at play, men sang songs on their way to work, families sang and played instruments together and with friends. Local bands were common, as we can see, for example, in the mines of Wales around the turn of the twentieth century. The south of Wales has a history of brass bands and singing. Each community might have had a band which would be called upon to play at local events. Instrumental skills were passed down from parent to child, or between community members. The Welsh Revival of 1904–1905 spawned many choirs, and their heritage of singing is still alive today. Every country had a heritage of folk music, especially those which had been touched by the gospel of Christ. This music of the common folk—the bands, choirs, and lullabies—was the true folk music. Melodies were used for decades, or centuries, in the enduring songs of the people.

The other track that music took in the twentieth century involved the professional composers who strove to make a statement in their music. Their music was often less melodic, less singable, less directly relevant to real life than was the music of the common people. Music moved closer toward atonality—that state where there is no home key to music—where, within some limitations, any note could be played in any chord. Dissonance abounds in music of this period—beauty is definitely not the primary goal of its composers. What a contrast to Bach's practice regarding dissonance: "… the dissonant [t]ones are written exclusively as passing tones, thus stressing the fundamental contrapuntal law that dissonances are permitted only on weak beats."[5] Bach employed dissonance rarely and in careful measure, using it to pass from one beautiful harmony to another.

As music changed from being overwhelmingly God-centred to being man-centred, it was transformed from something of beauty and order to a sound of chaos and disharmony. Those composers who proclaimed a faith in God generally created music with more order and pleasant harmonies, while those who declared themselves to be atheists, such as Bartok, sometimes produced atonal music that grated on the ear. Not all music was unpleasant, of course, just as not all musicians chose to rebel against God's created order. But there were certainly those composers who chose to buck the system, to create music that broke out of the boundaries which had been previously accepted in music. When this happened, the result was often confusion, rejection, and even violence in the audience. When we, from our vantage point in the 21st century, look back at the music that has been composed over the past several hundred years, our ears are so jaded that we cannot understand why the masses would have been so incensed when they were first exposed to these new sounds. Hundreds of years ago, before the invention of recording devices, the ears and minds of the populace were free from the constant bombardment of new and discordant sounds. They were accustomed to music being of an orderly and godly quality. Even after music lost much of its Christian connection, it still maintained the order and dignity of an earlier time. Therefore, when composers produced music that was disorderly, undignified, and raucous, it was a shock to the people of the time.

Prohibition was in force in the States from 1920 to1933, and during this time speakeasies came to be. These were music clubs where alcohol was sold illegally. The music which became popular in these clubs was jazz, a music form where rhythms are played out of square—the notes are unevenly divided. In other words, even if the music is written as eight eighth notes in a measure, each note does not have the same value in a measure of jazz music. Instead, the first eighth note in each set of two has twice the value of the last eighth note in that set, thereby making a sort of swinging tempo: daaa da daaa da daaa da daaa. "Jazz … was based on the beat of the voodoo drums of slaves during their religious ceremonies and rituals."[6] There are four or more subsets of jazz, including "the blues." When jazz music is accompanied by lyrics, the words used are sometimes just repeated nonsense syllables.

The intentions of the writers of jazz music were to decrease the inhibitions of its listeners; and as could be expected, the listeners became known as people with loose morals. Those who frequented the speakeasies of the time drank more than the government thought they ought to, and were often involved in flirting, table-top dancing, or extra-marital affairs. The music itself contributed to the moral breakdown of the times. "In 1924, when [George] Gershwin was twenty-five, Paul Whiteman, who wanted to make jazz respectable, commissioned Gershwin to write *Rhapsody in Blue*."[7] Notice that Whiteman wanted to make jazz respectable. It was not respectable—it contributed to riotous living. But Whiteman knew that if he could package jazz in a symphonic-type suite and play it in a concert hall, people would begin to think of jazz as an acceptable form of music. His plan worked.

The small groups of musicians providing music at the speakeasies of The Dirty Thirties grew into the big band music of the thirties and forties. In this style, a band consisted of ten or more brass, percussion, and saxophone players. This music was bigger and louder than the speakeasy jazz, and swing dancing became popular. This decade saw the percussion section become an integral part of the dance band. Our country and much of the western world went to war during this period, and servicemen were exposed to the music and morality of different cultures. Many children were fathered of North American servicemen, and women were brought home as war brides. The cultures of other nations began to infiltrate western culture in large measure. From pizza to Buddhism, from batik to the zither, many pieces of foreign culture were adopted into the Canadian mosaic and the American melting pot. Biblical discernment was generally ignored as we welcomed these new items into our lives; the desire for something new fueled their entrance. Some of these new cultural elements were amoral—that is, pizza is neither good nor evil, eaten in moderation. Buddhism, however, is obviously against the revealed truths of God. Batik can be made to decorate clothing in a pleasing way, with no moral objections. However, taking pagan music into our culture and church services could pose a problem. The prevalence of the radio just made the spread of foreign music that much more universal.

Enter the 1950's. This decade saw teenage rebellion become far more normalized as part of the culture and movie scene: *A Rebel Without a Cause* was produced in 1955 about troubled middle-class teenagers. This was the decade that saw the rise to popularity of Chuck Berry, Buddy Holly, and Elvis Presley. Music was turned on its head: instead of stressing the first and third beat, as had been the norm though the entirety of the history of written music, now popular music exhibited a heavy stress on beats two and four. This is the essence, the defining characteristic, of rock music.

> Mickey Hart of the Grateful Dead pointed out in a National Public Radio interview that accenting the 2nd and 4th beats in 4/4 time and accenting the 3rd beat in 3/4 time creates the backbeat which defines the essential and inherent core of rock music. The backbeat of rock, jazz, rap, swing, and other pagan styles is a violation of the Rule of Accent.[8]

Dan Peters and Steve Peters, in their book *Why Knock Rock?*, described rock music as sensual and rhythmic … steeped in rebellion.[9]

The preachers of the mid twentieth century warned about the folly of involvement in this type of entertainment. Even secular parents revolted against the rock music that was being listened to by the youth of that day. When that music eventually crept into the church, there was also an outcry among Christian parents.

Performed music became louder during the 1950's, and rock music remains a loud form of music today. A symphonic concert, during loud passages, registers 100–105 dB; a jackhammer three feet away is 110 dB; and 120 dB is the sound level of a jet engine heard on the runway from three hundred feet away—or of a typical rock concert.[10]

An interesting factor in the music of today is the prevalence of percussion instruments over any melodic or harmonic factors in the music. It's common to hear only the drum when your next door neighbour is playing his music too loudly, or to be bombarded with a repetitive drum or bass rhythm coming from the subwoofers of another car in traffic. The beat is driving and monotonous, and it has the effect of bringing out the baser nature of its listeners. I've walked through the mall and heard a band playing—or, at first, I thought it was a band. I heard the percussion, and assumed that when I got closer, I'd hear the rest of the music. But as I walked past the band, it was clear that there were only percussion instruments in the group. Monotonously their music droned on, beating a palpable rhythm in our chests as we walked by. The lack of melody, which appeals to the intellect, and harmony, which appeals to the soul, makes one wonder why the only thing left in this music was rhythm—which appeals to the body. Is it a coincidence that rap music, in which words are chanted rhythmically with no melody, is popular among violent gangs involved in crime? If we focus on "music" which is calling to our base, physical nature, we will feed that part of us that does not seek the higher things in life.

The lyrics of rock music, though using fewer meaningless words than the music of the thirties, often expressed the more negative side of human emotions: "I ain't nuthin' but a hound dog, cryin' all the time."[11] During the '50's promiscuity became more widespread, with boys making a distinction between "good girls" who wouldn't, and "nice girls" who would.

What is the purpose of the rock and roll music that developed in the 1950's? Its creators and performers have told us what they think, and many of their quotes can be found in the book Contemporary Christian Music Under the Spotlight. The goals of the purveyors of rock music are to interest people in sex, drugs, and a fleshly, rebellious lifestyle. Their desire is to motivate their listeners to licentious living. Is this simply done through the lyrics? If so, why couldn't they just change the words to Baroque tunes? It would not be as effective to proclaim the benefits of sleeping around to the tune of a Bach cantata.

Here are some quotes of some of the early purveyors of rock music.

> Rock 'n roll is synonymous with sex and you can't take that away from it. It just doesn't work.
> STEVEN TYLER OF AEROSMITH

I'm in rock music for the sex and narcotics.
GLENN FREY OF THE EAGLES

You can feel the adrenalin flowing through your body. It's sort of sexual. I entice my audience. What I do is very much the same as a girl's strip tease dance.
MICK JAGGER OF THE ROLLING STONES

I do deliver sex appeal. It's part of modern rock.
FREDDIE MERCURY OF QUEEN

Rock music is sex and you have to hit them in the face with it.
ANDREW OLDHAM, MANGER OF THE ROLLING STONES

This new genre of music created huge sensations in society. Parents were alarmed, teenagers were excited, and society shifted. Police started noticing violence that was common to rock music events.

Long before heavy metal and punk rock, simple, plain old rock and roll was considered a major threat to society. Certain radio DJs delighted in banning the music from their stations, while television personalities did much to try and limit the genre's popularity among teenagers. All efforts failed, of course. Before rock and roll's first decade was done, it was already the voice of a generation. Teenagers all across the world flocked to this new, high-speed rhythm with gusto. Most just wanted to dance, but a few wanted something a little extra.

In 1958, during an October show at the Ernst-Merck-Halle in Hamburg, West Germany, Bill Haley & His Comets—who are best remembered today for the ... song Rock Around the Clock—were busy performing when certain youths in attendance began picking fights with the Hamburg student association. Next, when about 100 police officers arrived, members of the crowd continued to throw punches and objects until the concert was terminated early. The Hamburg show cost some 20,000 deutsche marks in damage. Later that month, when Bill Haley and his band played at the Sportpalast in Berlin, another riot erupted that caused 50,000 deutsche marks in damage. The Berlin concert also proved to be more costly in terms of human health, for five police officers were badly beaten and six members of the audience were hospitalized.[12]

The fruit of the rough sensuality of 1950's music was the sexual revolution of the 1970's. The hippies staged love-ins and smoked marijuana to the tunes of the Beatles and the Beach Boys. It is no coincidence that many of those musicians became drug addicts. Jimi Hendrix, Janis Joplin, and Jim Morrison each died at age 27 of drug overdoses in the early 1970's, and there are many others who have shared a similar fate. They were reaping the fruit of their actions.

Popular music since those times has not improved in musicianship or morality. The styles have wended their way through various genres: hard rock, punk, screamo and metal have all voiced their angry protests to godly living. The words are a problem, to be sure; but I will seek, through the rest of this book, to show you that the music itself has a spiritual impact on its hearers. Music has formed the fall of our culture as surely as has any other earthly factor.

Popular music isn't the only form of music to have degraded markedly in the last century. Twentieth century music as performed in symphonic music halls is not much better than rock and roll.

> … humanism, leading to despair, has taken over much of music. My religion needs no God, only faith, said the philosophically orientated Schoenberg, and he placed great emphasis on expressing oneself.[13]

Schoenberg wrote atonal music which lacked melody or harmony, and was devoid of even a root to the scale. There was no home to his music—nothing to which the music resolved or gave a sense of peaceful completion. Other twentieth century composers joined Schoenberg in casting off as many musical conventions as they could, leading to a musical world lacking peace, stability, and beauty.

So with music in the orchestral world torn to shreds and music in the popular concert halls turned on its head, the only music remaining which was reliably good was in the churches. Chapter 8 tells the story of how church music was changed to be more like the world's music.

CHAPTER 5
A Biblical Argument

I cannot count how many times someone has asked me to prove from the Bible that rock music is evil. Nowhere in the Bible will you find the words "rock," "jazz," "hip hop," or "blues" mentioned in the context of music. To those who want the Bible to address their particular favourite form of music by name, I am patently unable to provide proof texts that rock music is wrong—and that closes the subject in their minds. To the person who is coming at the question of music from this point of view, I ask the corresponding question: Can you prove to me from the Bible that rock music is good?

The Bible was written over centuries, with the last book of our canon written near the end of the first century AD. Although principles addressing many of life's issues can be found in the Bible, modern inventions are conspicuously absent from its pages. And so, rock music is not mentioned in the Bible. Neither are cars, computers, or cocaine.

Since the style of rock music itself is not mentioned within the pages of Holy Scripture, we must be guided by the principles in the Bible which address music and godly living as we try to find out what God has in mind for us in the area of appropriate music.

If one wanted to find out from Scripture whether using heroin was an acceptable practice for Christians, searching "heroin" in the search bar would be fruitless. Instead, one would have to examine concepts like what God wants us to do with our bodies, our time, and our money. He tells us that our bodies are the temple of the Holy Ghost; that our time should be spent in useful pursuits, evangelism, godly fellowship, and healing rest; and that all of our money belongs to Him ultimately and our use of it should reflect that. We'd come across verses that tell us to not be drunk with wine, and we could apply that principle to drugs. We'd read that we are to be controlled by the Holy Spirit, and know that we should not give up bodily, emotional and spiritual control of ourselves to an addictive substance. And we would find in many places in the Bible that we are to reject and put to death our fleshly lusts, which war against the soul—and we would know that this applies to using illicit drugs.

Why is it so hard, then, to honestly examine what type of music we should listen to by using the principles God provides in the Bible? Are we compelled to admit that the Bible has nothing to say about styles of music, and therefore that we are free to listen to anything we like? To do so would be to believe the Bible uninspired, and God to be lacking knowledge, since He has not specifically addressed this or many other important modern topics.

II Peter 1:3–5 says,

> … his divine power hath given unto us all things that pertain unto life and godliness, through the knowledge of him that hath called us to glory and virtue: Whereby are given unto us exceeding great and precious promises: that by these ye might be partakers of the divine nature, having escaped the corruption that is in the world through lust. And beside this, giving all diligence, add to your faith virtue; and to virtue knowledge.

Here we see that God, in His infinite power and wisdom, has already given to us everything we need for life and godliness. If we need to know how to make musical standards, or standards in any area of life whose details are not directly addressed in the Bible, He has already given us what we need to make those choices. How are we to find this wisdom? This passage tells us that we have all things that pertain to life and godliness through the knowledge of him. The more we know God, the more able we'll be to discern between good and evil, and to sense His direction and calling. How do we know God? The primary way He has revealed Himself to us is through His written Word, the Bible. What has He called us to? He has called us to glory and virtue. He has called us to display His glory, and He has called us to virtue. Virtue is defined as behaviour showing high moral standards. Is there a difference in the moral standards shown in different forms of music? Excluding the lyrics, which are more objectively evaluated, can we truly judge music from a moral perspective? In the following chapters, I show that yes, we can evaluate music itself from a moral perspective—by its effects on people: both the current behaviour of those listening to it and reacting to its beat and the long-term effects, physical, emotional, and psychological, of those who make a habit of listening to different forms of music. We can also evaluate music's moral effects by the statements made about its purposes by its purveyors, and we can get some insight by viewing the lifestyles of those who create different kinds of music. Yes, music is a moral issue.

We are to be partakers of the divine nature. Although we are sinners, God has decreed that we should be the visible representations of Himself on this earth. We should be showing, not just by our conduct, but by our very beings, that we are partakers of the divine nature—we are God's own children. We are told, in this and other passages, to escape the corruption that is in the world through lust. What corruption? We can name obvious sins like murder and theft and call that the corruption of the world. We can go a little further and say that hate and selfishness are the corruption of the world. Knowing that the church has been accused by God of mixing with the world (see Revelation 2:14–16, 20–23, 3:2–4, I Corinthians 3:3–4, and all of I Corinthians chapters 5–8), we need to admit that the church struggles with the world's corruption. Here is God's exhortation in I John 2:15–16:

> Love not the world, neither the things that are in the world. If any man love the world, the love of the Father is not in him. For all that is in the world, the lust of the flesh, and the lust of the eyes, and the pride of life, is not of the Father, but is of the world.

Romans chapter 7 outlines quite clearly the struggle between our desire to be godly and the pull of the flesh. We know, through these passages and others, that every Christian must battle sinful desires in himself—none of us is above this. Now, on the one hand, we have escaped the corruption that is in the world through lust: that is, we have escaped the final consequence of being sinners (hell), and we have escaped from the identity we previously had: that of being children of the devil. Now, those who have trusted Christ as their Saviour from their sins are God's children! But we are still in a very current struggle to escape the corruption that is in the world, in the church, and in ourselves through lust. Lust is simply desire. *We want.* We don't always want things that are good for us. We want junk food, we want to stay up late, we want to take unwise risks, we want to disobey our authorities, we want things we can't afford—and the list goes on. When we are ruled by what we want instead of by what is good (which we should also want), we fall to the corruption of sin.

In Romans 8:13–14 we are warned,

> For if ye live after the flesh, ye shall die: but if ye through the Spirit do mortify the deeds of the body, ye shall live. For as many as are led by the Spirit of God, they are the sons of God.

As a related admonition, later in the same book we read,

> The night is far spent, the day is at hand: let us therefore cast off the works of darkness, and let us put on the armour of light. Let us walk honestly, as in the day; not in rioting and drunkenness, not in chambering and wantonness, not in strife and envying. But put ye on the Lord Jesus Christ, and make not provision for the flesh, to fulfil the lusts thereof. (Romans 13:12–14)

The rock music scene is certainly known by these elements: rioting, drunkenness, chambering, wantonness. As a matter of fact, my teenage son told me about a time he mentioned to his friends that he had been at a concert. Knowing our family's musical standards, his friends looked at him as if he had grown a second head. He explained that the Handel concert had been really good, but it had been quite late by the time he'd gotten to bed—around midnight. While they looked incredulously at him, he suddenly realized that their experiences with concerts were quite different than his experiences with concerts. He asked them what came to mind when they thought of the word "concert." They replied with statements like, "A big headache, because of lis-tening to such loud music," "Crowds," "Noise," "Up really late." These were Christian kids, who had experience going to concerts put on by Christian bands. The loud noises and high levels of emotional and sensory involvement were a stark contrast to the intense but peaceful emotions my son had felt at *The Messiah*.

At the end of the passage in I Peter 1, mentioned four pages ago, the writer tells us how we should be built up step by step. He says we are to add to our faith virtue. Again, virtue is "behaviour showing high moral standards." Does all music show high moral standards? It does not. The beauty and majesty of "The Hallelujah Chorus" cannot be compared to the products of 39 Stripes. Even before examining the components and effects of these types of music, we know that the feeling each produces is very different. In a Christian, "The Hallelujah Chorus" often produces a godly reverence, whereas the music of the other bands mentioned can produce agitation, sensuality, and a desire for fleshly pursuits. But more of that in a later chapter.

To virtue we are to add knowledge. I don't believe it was God's intent to restrict our growth in knowledge to solely biblical knowledge. Think of the advances of Christian scientists through the ages: men like Johannes Kepler, Sir Isaac Newton, Matthew Maury, Gregor Mendel, Russell Humphreys—men who, through their knowledge of God's Word, made great discoveries and developments in the physical world. All truth is God's truth. If we are to base our understanding of the physical realm on God's revealed Word, we will be able to agree with the Psalmist when he says,

O how love I thy law! it is my meditation all the day. Thou through thy commandments hast made me wiser than mine enemies: for they are ever with me. I have more understanding than all my teachers: for thy testimonies are my meditation. I understand more than the ancients, because I keep thy precepts. I have refrained my feet from every evil way, that I might keep thy word. I have not departed from thy judgments: for thou hast taught me. How sweet are thy words unto my taste! yea, sweeter than honey to my mouth! Through thy precepts I get understanding: therefore I hate every false way. (Psalm 119:97–104)

This book is all about adding to our faith knowledge in the area of music. Though there is much more to be learned about the subject of music and its effects on the human soul, in these pages I have tried to touch the relevant subjects regarding how music touches and transforms us. Knowledge in the realms of physiology, psychology, musicology, and other areas all point to the fact that music does indeed change us.

But before we get into discoveries about music shared by Christian and non-Christian scientists and musicians, let's talk about how to use Scripture to evaluate music. If the Bible does not mention rock music specifically—if there is no direct command about what type of music we should have on our smart phones, then how are we to use the Scripture to determine what is right to listen to? First of all, let's examine Hebrews 5:12–14.

> For when for the time ye ought to be teachers, ye have need that one teach you again which be the first principles of the oracles of God; and are become such as have need of milk, and not of strong meat. For every one that useth milk is unskilful in the word of righteousness: for he is a babe. But strong meat belongeth to them that are of full age, even those who by reason of use have their senses exercised to discern both good and evil.

This passage is talking about Christians who have been given what they needed to mature in their scriptural knowledge and spiritual maturity, and yet they are still babes. Little children need to be taught simple things in a concrete manner: we teach adding by playing with math manipulatives. High school students no longer need the manipulatives: instead, they are able to understand complex mathematical processes using abstract constructs. Baby Christians need everything spelled out for them. Mature Christians have, **by reason of use**, exercised **their senses** to discern both good and evil. Did you catch that? There are moral questions whose answers are not clearly spelled out in the Bible. For these situations, we need to practice using **our senses** to tell the difference between good and evil. Just as our noses can tell us when meat smells bad and shouldn't be eaten, and our eyes can tell us that our child looks sick, our ears can inform us as to the moral appropriateness of different forms of music. It takes practice! It takes learning. But these verses tell us that mature Christians are to study the things of this world, using their senses, under the scrutiny of God's Word, in order to discern between good and evil.

There are plenty of references in the Bible about music. Most of the verses concerning music are explicitly related to the worship of the Most High God. Over and over again we're told to sing a new song, to make a joyful and a skillful noise, to sing aloud to the God of our salvation. The music that was performed when the temple was built is mentioned in some detail. The words of one of the songs we'll sing in heaven are recorded in the book of Revelation. Besides these references about music used in the worship of God, though, there are some other uses mentioned.

We've discussed the children of Israel singing around the golden calf (Exodus 32:18). Job mentions that people had been singing songs about him to mock him.

> They were children of fools, yea, children of base men: they were viler than the earth. And now am I their song, yea, I am their byword. They abhor me, they flee far from me, and spare not to spit in my face. (Job 30:8–10)

In one of the Messianic songs, drunk people use music to mock the Lord. "I made sackcloth also my garment; and I became a proverb to them. They that sit in the gate speak against me; and I was the song of the drunkards." (Psalm 69: 11–12) Jeremiah was also mocked in song. "I was a derision to all my people; and their song all the day." (Jeremiah 3:14) In Psalm 137 we have an account of some of the captives of Israel, having been taken to Babylon, when their captors demanded them to sing praise songs to the Lord. They find themselves unable, in their grief, to sing those songs.

> For there they that carried us away captive required of us a song; and they that wasted us required of us mirth, saying, Sing us one of the songs of Zion. How shall we sing the LORD'S song in a strange land? (Psalm 137:3–4)

Wise King Solomon warns us not to be involved with the music of fools. "It is better to hear the rebuke of the wise, than for a man to hear the song of fools." (Ecclesiastes 7:5) Isaiah 23:15 mentions the song of the harlot.

The heathen are often recorded as singing about worldly things, such as in Ezekiel 27:25.

The Scripture commands us over and over again to sing to the Lord. These commands occur both in the Old Testament and in the New.

"Sing praises to the LORD, which dwelleth in Zion: declare among the people his doings." (Psalm 9:11)

> Let the Word of Christ dwell in you richly in all wisdom; teaching and admonishing one another in psalms and hymns and spiritual songs, singing with grace in your hearts to the Lord. (Colossians 3:16)

Believers are not restricted to only singing songs of praise to the Lord. In the Song of Solomon we see the mention of a love song. "Now will I sing to my wellbeloved a song of my beloved touching his vineyard." (Song of Solomon 5:1) In Genesis 31:27, Laban rebukes Jacob for leaving unannounced, by saying that he would have thrown him a farewell party, complete with songs, tabrets, and harps. The women of Israel sang about David slaying his ten thousands in I Samuel 18:7. Job recalls how his good works caused the widows to sing for joy. (Job 29:13)

There are many uses of music in the Bible, but by far the most commonly recorded reason for making music is to praise the Lord. But in the last several decades, people have used very different music to praise the Lord, and there have been sharp disagreements as to what kind of music is suitable for that purpose. Some state that music is amoral, and any music, within reason, will suffice for praise and worship songs. Others declare that some of the modern music is unsuitable for worshipping a holy God. Let's suppose for the purpose of discussion that there may be a difference between good and bad music. Let's assume that we, as Christians, armed with some knowledge and the Word of God, should be able to tell the difference between music we should and shouldn't be listening to; music that is appropriate for worship and that which is not. After all, most Christians do seem to recognize a line of some sort between music that they would find acceptable for a believer and music that is just too weird, dark, evil, or raunchy. If there is a moral quality in the music itself, how would the following verses apply to our study of music?

Take heed to thyself, lest thou make a covenant with the inhabitants of the land whither thou goest, lest it be for a snare in the midst of thee. (Exodus 34:12)

Thus saith the Lord: Learn not the way of the heathen. (Jer. 10:2)

I beseech you, therefore, brethren, by the mercies of God, that ye present your bodies a living sacrifice, holy, acceptable unto God, which is your reasonable service. **And be not conformed to this world**: but be ye transformed by the renewing of your mind, that ye may prove what is that good, and acceptable, and perfect, will of God. (Romans 12:1–2)

Be ye not unequally yoked together with unbelievers: for what fellowship hath righteousness with unrighteousness? and what communion hath light with darkness? And what concord hath Christ with Belial? or what part hath he that believeth with an infidel? And what agreement hath the temple of God with idols? for ye are the temple of the living God; as God hath said, I will dwell in them, and walk in them; and I will be their God, and they shall be my people. Wherefore come out from among them, and be ye separate, saith the Lord, and touch not the unclean thing; and I will receive you, And will be a Father unto you, and ye shall be my sons and daughters, saith the Lord Almighty. Having therefore these promises, dearly beloved, **let us cleanse ourselves from all filthiness of the flesh and spirit, perfecting holiness in the fear of God.** (II Corinthians 6:14–7:1)

Love not the world, neither the things that are in the world. If any man love the world, the love of the Father is not in him. (I John 2:15)

The verses above tell us that we are to leave behind the things of the world when we become a Christian. We are not to walk as they walk, to act as they act, to revel in what they revel in. That doesn't mean that we're to be different just so that we're different. No, it means that in following Christ, we are going in the opposite direction from the world, and that should show in our behaviour. As we'll learn in another chapter, the roots of rock music, Christian or not, come from the world. It was not invented for the bride of

Christ. In taking CCM into the church, we have brought something that was invented by the world, for the world, into the sanctuary, to be used in the worship of the living God. Now, the form of music itself is a different issue from the technical elements of corporate worship. We use electric lights and video projectors; these things were never used in King David's time. It's not the physical aids that make the biggest difference in how we worship, but the actual music used. The music we are using in the church today indisputably found it origins in the music of the world. Think about that in context of the above verses. We are to add to virtue knowledge—and yet, in Hosea 4:6, God says that His people are destroyed for lack of knowledge. We as God's redeemed people need to add to our virtue knowledge, so that we can continue to reflect His image accurately to a lost and dying world. We are to be careful to maintain the purity of our hearts and souls.

> Only take heed to thyself, and **keep thy soul diligently**, lest thou forget the things which thine eyes have seen, and lest they depart from thy heart all the days of thy life: but teach them thy sons, and thy sons' sons. (Deuteronomy 4:9)

> Keep thy heart with all diligence; for out of it are the issues of life. (Proverbs 4:23)

> The heart is deceitful above all things, and desperately wicked: who can know it? (Jeremiah 17:9)

> We are to fight against the lust that strives for mastery in us.

> Now these things were our examples, to the intent we should not lust after evil things, as they also lusted. Now all these things happened unto them for ensamples: and they are written for our admonition, upon whom the ends of the world are come. Wherefore let him that thinketh he standeth take heed lest he fall. (I Corinthians 10: 6, 11, 12)

> This I say then, Walk in the Spirit, and ye shall not fulfil the lust of the flesh. For the flesh lusteth against the Spirit, and the Spirit against the flesh: and these are contrary the one to the other: so that ye cannot do the things that ye would. (Galatians 5:16–17)

And they that are Christ's have crucified the flesh with the affections and lusts. (Galatians 5:24)

This I say therefore, and testify in the Lord, that ye henceforth walk not as other Gentiles walk, in the vanity of their mind, having the understanding darkened, being alienated from the life of God through the ignorance that is in them, because of the blindness of their heart: Who being past feeling have given themselves over unto lasciviousness, to work all uncleanness with greediness... That ye put off concerning the former conversation the old man, which is corrupt according to the deceitful lusts; and be renewed in the spirit of your mind; and that ye put on the new man, which after God is created in righteousness and true holiness. (Ephesians 4:17–24)

Flee also youthful lusts: but follow righteousness, faith, charity, peace, with them that call on the Lord out of a pure heart. (II Timothy 2:22)

Wherefore gird up the loins of your mind, be sober, and hope to the end for the grace that is to be brought unto you at the revelation of Jesus Christ; As obedient children, **not fashioning yourselves according to the former lusts in your ignorance**: But as he which hath called you is holy, so be ye holy in all manner of conversation; Because it is written, Be ye holy; for I am holy. (1 Peter 1:13–16)

Dearly beloved, I beseech you as strangers and pilgrims, abstain from fleshly lusts, which war against the soul. (I Peter 2:11)

The passage in Ephesians 4, mentioned on the previous page, says that lust is deceitful. We desire certain things so strongly that we convince ourselves they are all right. Christians living in the southern US more than a century ago convinced themselves that keeping slaves was okay. Some Christians in 21st century Canada have convinced themselves that it's fine to have abortions. We don't tend to make decisions based on logic, but on what we want. More on that in Chapter 11.

Everything we do has an impact on who we are. Our choices help to form what we believe.

Can a man take fire in his bosom, and his clothes not be burned? (Proverbs 6:27)

Be not deceived; God is not mocked: for whatsoever a man soweth, that shall he also reap. For he that soweth to the flesh shall of the flesh reap corruption; but he that soweth to the Spirit shall of the Spirit reap life everlasting. (Galatians 6:7–8)

Be not deceived: evil communications corrupt good manners. (I Corinthians 15:33)

It would be naive to assume that just because some Christians participate in an activity, it must be right. Even if most Christians we know enjoy something, that doesn't make it right. And when Christian pastors and elders begin to commend something which they previously forbade, our ears should perk up as we attempt, through the Word of God and the facts He brings to our knowledge, to discern between good and evil.

Beware of false prophets, which come to you in sheep's clothing, but inwardly they are ravening wolves. Ye shall know them by their fruits. (Matthew 7:15–16a)

Your glorying is not good. Know ye not that a little leaven leaveneth the whole lump? (I Corinthians 5:6)

Pure religion and undefiled before God and the Father is this: to visit the poor and widows in their affliction, and to **keep himself unspotted from the world**. (James 1:27)

Whatsoever things are true, whatsoever things are honest, whatsoever things are just, whatsoever things are pure, whatsoever things are lovely, whatsoever things are of good report; if there be any virtue, and if there be any praise, think on these things. (Philippians 4:8)

Since we have these promises, beloved, let us cleanse ourselves from all filthiness of the flesh and spirit, **perfecting holiness in the fear of God**. (2 Corinthians 7:1)

… be diligent that ye may be found of him in peace, without spot, and blameless. (II Peter 3:14)

(All **bold** emphases in the above Scripture references are mine.)

Some of the above verses have something to say about not being like the world, but instead, being like our Father, God. How can a Christian be like the world? Well, there are certain ways we need to be like the world in order to reach the world for Christ. We need to speak the same language as those we hope to reach. Since eating together is such an important part of human fellowship, it's a good thing to learn proper manners and to learn to eat the food of the people to whom you are ministering, or with whom you are living. We need to make sure that the productive part of our lives—our jobs—are actually useful to the people around us. For instance, Paul was a tent maker. He constructed useful products in order to serve those around him and make a living. With this living, he was able to maintain himself well enough that he could preach the gospel. Those things are important ways that we really ought to be like the world.

But, should we be like the world in our enjoyments? In some tribes, it is a normal, enjoyable thing for the men of the tribe, or at least the elders, to gather together when a girl reaches menarche and each, in turn, defile her. Obviously this is not something a Christian would take part in. It is normal in our society for people to watch movies with swearing in them. Even children's movies contain profanity. It's normal for adults to watch "adult" movies, and it's quite common for men, and some women, to enjoy pornography. Where do we as Christians draw the line? If there are no movies without profanity, should we just watch those with as little profanity as we can find? Or should we throw that standard to the wind, and watch whatever is popular in the culture? Perhaps there is a third option: watch only movies that have no profanity, either by design or by editing; or, even more shockingly, watch no movies, if no decent ones can be found. *Is entertainment so necessary* that we will put up with sin in order to be entertained? What happened to the Psalmist's vow, "I will set no wicked thing before mine eyes: I hate the work of them that turn aside; it shall not cleave to me."? (Psalm 101:3)

In the same vein, why should Christians listen to godly music? As we'll find in the following chapters, music actually changes our brains. The music of the world has been a very integral part of the cultural revolution that has taken place in recent decades: why again is it that we should welcome this music of cultural and personal transformation into our churches? How much like the world's music should the music of the church be? Where do we draw the line? Should a line be drawn?

There are those who will tell you that whatever is done "to the Lord" is acceptable to the Lord. I tell you with tears in my eyes that these people are sincerely wrong. Over and over again in Scripture we see that some people were more involved in the offering than they were concerned about truly pleasing God. In Numbers 16 we read the account of Korah, Dathan, and Abiram, who didn't like the spiritual leadership that God had set up and thought they could do a better job. They perished as a result of their rebellion. Nadab and Abihu, sons of the high priest Aaron, decided to offer "strange fire before the Lord, which he commanded them not." They took the elements of the pure worship of the true God, and knowingly put them together in the wrong way: they were killed for it. (Leviticus 10:1–2) And then there were the Pharisees, who tithed mint and cumin but ignored the weightier matters of the law. (Matthew 23:23) Jesus rejected their spiritual leadership, calling them the blind leading the blind. (Luke 6:39) Some of these people were using sacrifices that God had permitted; some were not. Some seemed to truly believe in their hearts that they were sacrificing to the Lord when they were really, by God's estimation, in rebellion against Him. Hear what God says about those who think they're sacrificing to Him, when they're really offering something He finds abominable.

> I hate, I despise your feast days, and I will not smell in your solemn assemblies. Though ye offer me burnt offerings and your meat offerings, I will not accept them: neither will I regard the peace offerings of your fat beasts. Take thou away from me the noise of thy songs; for I will not hear the melody of thy viols. But let judgment run down as waters, and righteousness as a mighty stream. (Amos 5:21–24)

> To what purpose is the multitude of your sacrifices unto me? saith the LORD … Bring no more vain oblations; incense is an abomination unto me; the new moons and sabbaths, the calling of assemblies, I cannot away with; it is iniquity, even the solemn meeting. Your new moons and your appointed feasts my soul hateth: they are a

trouble unto me; I am weary to bear them. And when ye spread forth your hands, I will hide mine eyes from you: yea, when ye make many prayers, I will not hear: your hands are full of blood. Wash you, make you clean; put away the evil of your doings from before mine eyes; cease to do evil; Learn to do well; seek judgment, relieve the oppressed, judge the fatherless, plead for the widow.

Come now, and let us reason together, saith the LORD: though your sins be as scarlet, they shall be as white as snow; though they be red like crimson, they shall be as wool. If ye be willing and obedient, ye shall eat the good of the land: But if ye refuse and rebel, ye shall be devoured with the sword: for the mouth of the LORD hath spoken it. (Isaiah 1:11)

Saul was the first king of Israel. Chosen by God, he started out well, apparently humble and unassuming. However, he quickly conformed to the desires of the people. When Samuel told him God's command to completely kill all the Amalekites and their livestock, he decided to please the people instead of obeying God. He saved alive Agag, the king of Amalek, and he reserved many of the best of the livestock—he said they had been reserved for sacrifice to the Lord. The prophet Samuel found Saul and asked him about the livestock. Instead of admitting that he had sinned in disobeying God, Saul justified his actions. To this Samuel replied, Hath the Lord as great delight in burnt offerings and sacrifices, as in obeying the voice of the Lord? Behold, to obey is better than sacrifice, and to hearken than the fat of rams. (I Samuel 15:22) Saul lost God's favour and his future dynasty because of his rebellion. He had thought that his sacrifice would be acceptable to God. But under God's specific command to Saul, he was to kill all the livestock, not save it for sacrifice. This changing of God's stated command had serious repercussions for Saul.

In the eighth chapter of Ezekiel, we see the elders of Israel making sacrifices to false gods in the temple. Why did they defile the temple with these sacrifices? Couldn't they have sacrificed to their pagan deities somewhere else? They recognized the importance of the temple as a place of worship, and so chose that place to offer their abominable sacrifices.

Today, the music that is presented before God's people often resembles the music of worldly dances and bars more than that of godly believers offering praise to the Most High. Performers of CCM will tell you that since they are dedicating their music to the Lord, the Lord will bless the efforts of their hearts. They often truly believe that what they are doing is right and holy. But does the action of offering something to the Lord make that object (or song) acceptable to Him? I don't believe we have scriptural ground for saying it does. The sacrifices of the world have come into the temple—and the church will be held accountable.

CHAPTER 6

What's the Big Deal about Beat and Syncopation?

Let's carry on, now, from our overview of the history of music, to music as it has been recorded on paper, vinyl, or silicone from long ago until the present time. Written music can now indicate not only the pitch and rhythm of the notes, but also the tempo, dynamics, articulation, and mood.

When we listen to music of any sort, we may find our toes tapping, our heads nodding, or we may walk in time to the song. Music is naturally divided into beats—but what is a beat? Think of yourself taking a long walk on a smooth walking trail. Your feet fall naturally in a regular pattern. Imagine, as you walk, singing a song such as *Jesus Loves Me*. If you sing a new syllable on each footfall, you are walking on the beat.

A beat is, basically, a measure of time in music. Each beat in a piece of simple music should last for exactly the same length of time as all the other beats. Modern music is divided into measures, each of which contain a given number of beats. Separated by bar lines, one measure contains the same number of beats and occupies the same amount of time as any other measure in that section of music. For instance, let's say that each measure in 4/4 time lasts for 4 seconds. That means that since there are 4 beats in each measure, each beat will last for one second. So, we could count 1–2–3–4 while keeping in time with a watch or clock. If we repeated the numbers 1 to 4 over and over again, in time with the passing of seconds, we would be counting out the beats of the music.

Most western music is written in 4/4 time. That time signature indicates that there are four beats in each measure and each quarter note (♩) receives one beat. So common is this time signature that we have come to call it common time. Since each measure of music written in 4/4 time has four beats, any measure could include four quarter notes or any of the other endless combinations of notes which can, together, add up to four beats. When music is played, we can recognize the time signature by the subtle stresses placed on the different beats of the music. Beat one has always been the strongest of the beats in Western music. The beat next in strength is beat 3. Beats 2 and 4 are weak beats. To represent the beats in written form, they would look like this: **1**–2–**3**–4. For centuries of written music, we have accepted that orderly music is written by stressing the first beat in each measure, and the third beat in 4/4 time is played more strongly than beats 2 and 4. This method of stressing the first and third beat in each measure of 4/4 time lends itself to a feeling of stability and order. Throughout all of the history of music, as long as there has been 4/4 time, as long as music has been written down, this has been the accepted order and beauty of music in common time.

The crucial notes in the melody are often played on beat 1, and when words accompany the music, the most important words are usually placed on beat 1. Important words and notes are placed on beat three as well, since it is the second strongest beat. Beats two and four fill time, keep things regular, and give a contrast to the strong beats. Just as when we speak, we naturally emphasize certain words and syllables, so it is in music. If we were to always talk with the same amount of emphasis on each syllable, we would say that we were speaking in a monotone. In a very similar way, music is made up of a dance of stressed and unstressed notes that help to tell a story. The orderly rhythm of music has been an expression of the onward march of a healthy society.

Until the 20th century. In the first half of the 1900's, things changed. Whereas Western society, based on Christian morals, had encouraged respect for one's elders, for law and order, and for treating one's fellow man with care, in the 20th century, these normative values began to erode. Respect for parents was traded in for an overdependence on one's peers. Law and order began to be taken more lightly. From the speakeasies of the '30's to the rock concerts of the '50's, young people began to experience a culture vastly different from the ones in which their grandparents had grown up. And at the core of this widespread cultural shift was music which cast off the bonds of the previous generations.

In the early 1950's, a form of music became popular in which the traditionally stressed beats of 4/4 time were reversed, to create a sound which was totally different from almost all previously written music. The defining quality of rock music is that the stresses of the beats are changed, and that change is usually emphasized in the percussion section. Typically, there will be an accompaniment which plays 1–**2**–3–**4** in rock music. The melody will often have some emphasis on beat 1, but will also lean toward stressing beats 2 and 4.

Now, you may say, "What difference does it make which beats are emphasized? What's the big deal? The beat is not an entity in itself, but simply an element of music." Yes, the beat is an element of music. Let me draw a parallel. Letters are amoral. I cannot express good or evil by simply saying, "a." As a matter of fact, the letter b has no greater value than the letter t. Letters themselves are amoral—without moral effect. However, the purpose of letters is to be combined into words, and the words into sentences, paragraphs, essays, books, love letters and grocery lists. These words have power to convince, to change people's minds, to influence people to do good or to do evil. We use the simple elements of language to express thoughts with which we make an impact on others.

Pythagoras, a mathematician and philosopher of the fifth century BC, taught that music was composed of three parts: melody, which appealed to the mind of man; harmony, which spoke to the spirit of man; and rhythm, which moved the body of man. These three simple elements of music—melody, harmony, and rhythm, can be put together to create musical thoughts which can and do have an impact on their listeners. Language is more cerebral, and we can track down where we came up with certain thoughts or ideas. It's harder to measure the impact of music because it speaks directly to the soul.

However, since music does show its effects on our bodies and minds, we can also seek to estimate its impact on the soul.

The throwing off of the morals of previous generations corresponded with the accepted rules of music being thrown out in the early parts of the twentieth century. Truly the music world was turned on its head when musicians like the Beatles, The Monkeys, and Elvis Presley began to rock the foundations of musical sense by stressing the beats which heretofore had been unstressed, and relieving the stressed beats of their importance. The message they were sending was undeniably clear to the adults who were listening: "We are rejecting your rules and your morals. We will make our own way in this world. We will do it our way, and we *will not* submit ourselves to anyone's rules." Given that the stated purpose of rock musicians is to promote rebellion, sex, and drugs, this turned-around music was a very effective medium by which to attain their goals. Imagine, if you can, living all your life listening to the music of brilliant musicians like Bach and Handel, Beethoven and Mozart, and suddenly having all the rules of music changed. Certainly you would take notice. The Christian and secular parents of the 1950's recognized the rock and roll music of the times as evil. They reacted strenuously against it, but their protests had little effect. Since the young people had decided to rebel, they surely wouldn't be listening to their parents' antiquated ideas of what music should sound like. The youth wanted to listen to the new music, which appealed to their senses like no other music ever had.

And surely it did. All of us recognize that music has a powerful impact on our emotions. Take away the music from a suspenseful movie, and it grows boring. Remove the music from a funny movie and it becomes less humorous. Take the sound track from the action flick and suddenly the story loses its drive. We know that music can lead some people to tears. Music has been used to drum up patriotism or to torture its hearers. Music in the middle of the twentieth century fed the fleshly desires of the youth who attended the rock concerts. The contrast between this music and the music that had been listened to in previous generations was astonishing.

In addition to the disruption of the strong beats in music, another hallmark characteristic of rock, and of CCM, is syncopation. But what exactly is syncopation? According to Wikipedia, "syncopation involves a variety of rhythms which are in some way unexpected, which make part or all of a tune or piece of music off-beat." We can define the term "off-beat" as simply being rhythms which happen at a different time than exactly on any beat. So, if a note is played halfway between beats 1 and 2, we might say that note is off-beat. But considering the fact that, for most of the recorded history of music, beats 1 and 3 have been the stressed beats in 4/4 time, we could also say that music which stresses beats 2 and 4 repeatedly is off-beat, or syncopated.

If syncopation is any unexpected rhythm which happens on off beats, then we can say that Bach, Handel, and Haydn all used syncopation. There are often unexpected rhythmic elements in their music. As a matter of fact, when J.S.Bach was hired to be the organist in the town of Halle, his job contract stipulated that he

> accompany attentively the regular chorales and those prescribed by the minister ... slowly and without embellishment, in four and five part, ... as well as syncopations and suspensions, in such a manner that the congregation can take the organ as the basis of good harmony and unison tone.[1]

Here, Bach is specifically requested to use syncopations. What did the church board of Halle mean by these syncopations? Well, given my knowledge of how church pianists today accompany the congregation, I would expect that they meant that the melody and harmony of the chorale itself would be embellished with in-between notes—notes between the notes of the melodic line that would beautify the music and keep the congregation in tune and in time as they sang. What, then, is the difference between the unexpected rhythms of Bach and the syncopation of popular music today?

Bach was a master of music. He was fluent in writing, composing, and performing music on the organ, the violin, or with the orchestra. He had a prolific output of original music. He was the musician who formalized what we now know as the major and minor keys of music when he wrote *The Well-Tempered Clavier*. While Bach is not everyone's cup of tea, there are few Bach compositions that a reasonably well-educated music lover would call truly boring. He used the element of surprise occasionally in his music, and his rhythms are marvelously complex. He is known for depth in counterpoint and harmony. Within the context of a piece of music that is well-founded in strong, traditional use of 4/4 or 3/4 time, he would occasionally create a rhythm that was not as strongly on the beat as would normally be expected. He used this rhythm to briefly take the listener to a place of imbalance—and then he returned them to stable rhythms once again. The syncopation of this kind of music is a brief departure from regular, predictable beats, which then returns to the expected musical stresses. This brief departure does not characterize the rhythm of the music, but remains as a minor player in the composition. This attitude towards regular rhythms and sparse syncopation is common throughout all Baroque musicians and most of the musicians from the Classic period and beyond. Syncopation was used to add variety, but it was usually added for a purpose. In Vivaldi's "Credo" (RV591), for instance, the composer used syncopation to make a particular phrase stand out. He also used complexity in rhythm and melody to point out the great mystery of God becoming man in Christ. Thus rhythm was used to communicate thoughts in music.

The rhythms of today's music are a stark contrast to what Bach, Beethoven, and Brahms composed. When modern music is written exactly as it is performed, the resultant notation is so complex as to be almost impossible to accurately read and performed by the average musician. With today's technology, one can sing into a microphone and a computer will notate exactly what was sung. Musicians can belt out any rhythm they like, and the computer will be able to analyze and print the rhythm. So many of the notes occur off the beat—any beat—that there are constant ties and dots. These ties and dots are rhythmic shorthand which make it possible to communicate intricate rhythms. However, the over-abundance of them in modern song-writing leads to a situation where almost no notes happen on the beat at all and it's very difficult to play the rhythm exactly as written. Much music played by worship teams today is learned by ear because the written notes would be too hard to learn. Instead of the syncopation that would be typical of one of the masters, which gives a brief period of rhythmic instability resolving quickly to a settled rhythm, the music heard on the radio or in many churches today is *more syncopated than not*, and never resolves to a place of rhythmic stability. These songs can only be sung by the average listener if he is familiar with the pieces from having heard them on the radio, or on his device, or at church, many times before attempting to sing them.

Tim, a friend who leads music at his church, brought his guitar over to my house. He told me about a song he was learning. He had asked the music leader for the sheet music to this particular song. Tim was given the lyrics with the chords written above the words. This is a common way of writing guitar music, but he needed to know how to rhythmically coordinate his chording with the lyrics, and how to sing them. When he asked the person who had introduced the song what the rhythm was, he was told to just play it as he felt it—to not worry about what the rhythm was. This is because today's CCM rhythms don't make a lot of sense to amateur musicians, and are so complex that it would not be an effective use of time to learn each rhythm precisely. Therefore, variations in rhythm are made to CCM songs in many churches. Singing primarily off-beat songs in a rhythm known to no one but the song leader makes these melodies frustrating and difficult for the congregation to sing.

This syncopated music keeps one in a constant state of musical imbalance. At our ministry, when we have tried to introduce music with rhythms that are somewhat unpredictable, the result is that almost none of the children will sing along, and none learn it well. We don't hear these more complicated songs being sung while children wait for a meal or an activity, and it is seldom requested at song time. If there were a recording they could listen to multiple times, they would learn it—particularly if it were performed by their favourite band! But it proves to be just too hard to learn to sing when the rhythms are complex. Therefore, in the interest of encouraging participation, we stick to songs with predictable rhythms—songs without much syncopation or very unpredictable rhythms. The children and youth pick up the tunes for these songs quickly, often by the second or third verse. They sing them while they are getting their meals or on the way to activities, and we even hear them sing these songs when they return for later events! The truths of God embed themselves in the hearts and minds of these participants because we give them singable, learnable songs to solidify the concepts in their hearts. Congregational singing in churches would improve markedly if church musicians would follow this policy of using mostly unsyncopated music. There are other reasons for using songs with rhythms that are primarily on the beat, but the need for congregations to be able to quickly learn a piece of music that can carry them through the week is a strong argument against syncopation.

Jane Stuart Smith and Betty Carlson give a more detailed definition of syncopation in their description of ragtime music in the book *The Gift of Music*. They write,

> In ragtime, as in jazz, what makes its distinctive rhythm is the way the melody line is set against the bass line; that is, the melodic note is delayed or advanced for half a beat or for an eighth note while the left hand is kept steady. This is syncopation, or you could say, ragged time.[2]

This is exactly what you see in much CCM music today: the drum or piano gives a constant, steady beat, while the melodic instruments or the singer presents a melody whose emphases do not correspond with the underlying beat. Notes may happen on the off-beat (2 or 4), on an eighth note (in between any two beats), or they may just happen at any time. A stark contrast to syncopated music, though, would be music that is only played right on the beat—so, four equal notes in each measure of music in 4/4 time, for instance. Some good music is written just like this. However, since most composers do not have the musical genius of Bach or Beethoven, if we were to restrict all music to only have new notes start right on the beat—that would be boring! I know of no one who contends that writing eighth notes between the beats is wrong. I believe it's the balance of the thing. Are most words in a song happening *off* the beat? Then we can call that music syncopated. Are most words, or at least the stressed words or syllables, happening *on* the beat? Then that music is not what we would call syncopated.

The language form that is closest to music is poetry. In poetry we do not simply state a concrete thought, but with carefully chosen words we evoke images and emotions. These words are chosen, not just for their meaning, but also for their sound—the way their letters and accents blend together with the other words in the poem to paint a musical picture in our minds. Traditional poetry is arranged in lines containing a certain number of syllables, with a predetermined pattern of stresses, or accents. The words that we want to emphasize are placed in a stressed position in the line. This verse of a poem by T. S. Eliot clearly shows the regularity of the stresses placed on every third syllable.

Gus, the Theater Cat

Gus is the Cat at the Theatre Door.
His name, as I ought to have told you before,
Is really Asparagus.
That's such a fuss
To pronounce, that we usually call him just Gus.[3]

The words of most hymns are written as poetry before being set to music. They make sense on their own as poems with rhyme and rhythm. The music added to them is meant to give beauty and meaning, and to unite the worshippers as they sing together the praises of God. The hymn writer takes the lyrics and sets them to music so that the important words are stressed. He places the crucial words on strong beats of the music, and places small or unimportant words, such as articles and prepositions (the, an, in, on), as well as unaccented syllables, on short notes and off-beat notes. Multi-syllabic words are given a place in the melody where their natural stresses fall on the stronger beats. This leads to a fluidity of song, with the meanings of the words emphasized by the music.

In modern music, there is little predictability. Whereas the words of a hymn would work well as a poem, words from some modern songs are unnecessarily repetitious, unpoetic, and disorganized. Words can happen anywhere, on any beat, or more likely, between beats. In the typical hymn, accented syllables and important words are placed on stressed beats; in syncopated music, words can be placed at any point in the measure. By the end of the twentieth century, most CCM seemed to be composed of rhythms that contained more off-the-beat words than on-the-beat words. Around 2010, an interesting twist in the development of over-syncopation occurred: in new CCM songs, the name of God was now most commonly presented as an off-the-beat word. Consider again the fact that, in poetry, important words are placed at a position of strength in the line. To place a word at a position of weakness communicates that it is not an important word. Therefore, to place God's name (in Christian music, no less!) repeatedly at a place of non-stress in music communicates, whether consciously or unconsciously, that He is not that important after all.

How does one explain something that is spiritually discerned? It's not as easy as describing a physical object. Even Jesus, while conversing with Nicodemus in John 3, didn't take time to explain the intricacies of how the Holy Spirit works. He said, "The wind bloweth where it listeth, and thou hearest the sound thereof, but canst not tell whence it cometh, and whither it goeth: so is every one that is born of the Spirit." What Jesus is explaining here is that, while our finite minds cannot understand in detail the Person of the Holy Spirit, we can see His *effects* in the lives of those around us, and even in ourselves. And so, as we consider the question of how syncopated music appeals to our sensual, fleshly natures, it is beyond my ability to fully explain the method by which the Holy Spirit moves us, nourishes us, and builds us up with good, godly music—or how Satan attracts us, deceives us, and destroys our attempts at holiness when we fill our lives with fleshly music. But we can observe the behaviours of those who listen to sensual music, and through our observations, learn its *effects*. As we develop discernment in this area, we may be able to feel the effects of different types of music on our own bodies, souls, and spirits.

First, let's consider the lifestyles of those heavily involved in carnal music. The lifestyles of rock and jazz musicians tend to be rife with sexual affairs, broken marriages, drug use, alcohol, and other forms of promiscuity. These things are typical of those who spend a great portion of their time perform-ing sensual music—and to a somewhat lesser extent, those who frequently listen to this type of music. And CCM artists are not far removed from this sort of lewd lifestyle. Many CCM musicians have been involved in drugs, extra-marital sex, and other forms of ungodly sensuality. Why is that? Could it really be a coincidence that so many of these people who are held up as heroes by many in the church today are not living a godly lifestyle? Instead, I think we must admit that the music which is their livelihood influences them in a negative direction.

Then, let's look at the immediate effect of syncopation on the bodies of the people listening to it. Even in church, you will find people moving their bodies in dancing, swaying motions while the worship team performs. They are touched, sure—their emotions are intensified by the music. They think that these heightened emotions are due to spiritual experiences. But are these spiritual experiences resulting in what God desires?

Isaiah 66:1–4 reads:

> Thus saith the Lord: Heaven is My throne, and the earth is My footstool. Where is the house that ye build unto Me? and where is the place of My rest? For all those things hath mine hand made, and all those things have been, saith the Lord: But to this man will I look: even to him that is poor and of a contrite spirit, and trembleth at My word. He that killeth an ox is as if he slew a man; he that sacrificeth a lamb, as if he cut off a dog's neck; he that offereth an oblation, as if he offered swine's blood; he that burneth incense, as if he blessed an idol. Yea, they have chosen their own ways, and their soul delighteth in their abominations. I also will choose their delusions, and will bring their fears upon them; because when I called, none did answer; when I spake, they did not hear: but they did evil before mine eyes, and chose that in which I delighted not.

Here we see that the people of Israel were doing the things that they thought God required of them: they had a temple, they made blood sacrifices according to the Law, they offered grain and tithes of all, they burned incense and followed the letter of the Old Testament Law. But that was not what God wanted. He wanted, and had already expressed that He wanted, a contrite spirit which trembled at His Word. He wanted repentance, humility, and submission. He wanted a sincere respect for the Word He had given. Instead, the Israelites built themselves up in their own minds, believing their sacrifices and behaviour to be making them important to God.

Are we, the North American church, living the same way? Do our worship teams make themselves important as they artfully perform syncopated songs for the audience? Are there those who are steeped in worldly musical practices while singing words of holiness? Are there some whose way of life is an abomination to God, yet who hold themselves up as examples of love and tolerance?

Does promoting music that encourages sensuality really glorify God? I think not.

CHAPTER 7
Our Changing World

I grew up in the country, on a five-acre parcel of land nestled between farms in a beautiful valley. Life was different then. Families were larger. There were five children in our family, and that was pretty typical in our community. Everyone lived with their own mother, father, and siblings. Everyone ate meals with their families, and all children went to public school. Each school day was begun with the students standing while the principal recited the Lord's prayer over the intercom. Many, if not most, of our friends and neighbours went to a church of some kind, and almost everyone professed a belief in God. I didn't know anyone who became pregnant outside of marriage until a classmate dropped out of high school to hide her pregnancy in our graduating year. When my parents separated the summer before my graduating year, my life was suddenly thrown into a tailspin. Ours had not been a happy family, but to have one parent suddenly opt out was a crushing blow. I told no one. It was summer vacation, and I didn't live near most of my friends. Cell phones had not been invented, and I rarely used the house phone. When school went back in session, I just didn't mention it. No one I knew had parents who had separated—I didn't even know how to broach the topic. Several months later I found out that the parents of a close friend had also separated, so I told her about my own family break-up. She and I were the only people I knew personally who had experienced parental divorce or separation.

While sin has always been a major force in every human culture, in the society in which I grew up the grossest displays of it were held back by the cultural mores of the time. In my great-grandparents' generation, most marriages lasted a lifetime, and homosexuality was basically unheard of in common society. My great-grandparents were married for 67 years. They survived an intercontinental move, separation from family, poverty while homesteading in a new land just before and during the Great Depression, and multiple hardships, all while raising nine children. When my great-grandmother had one of her frequent "sick headaches," my gruff old great-grandfather would make her a cup of tea and encourage her to rest until the migraine passed. They were faithful to each other for life. All of their children married, and most, if not all, of them were totally monogamous. However, the changing morals in Canadian society was reflected in our family. Over the years we have lost the heritage of faithful, long-term marriages, and the lifestyles of my extended family now reflect the morals of the twenty-first century.

Contrast the lifestyle of my great-grandparents with today's TV fare, which shows LGBTQ couples on many prime time shows. Divorce and remarriage are common in movies and sitcoms. The stories of traditional families that my generation learned about in our school readers are vastly different than the dogma that is being taught to our kindergarteners today: that any configuration of family is just fine.

In our ministry we deal with children from all walks of life. From the spoiled princess with the latest gadgets to the foster kid with minimal belongings, we see them all. These days, it is unusual to discover that one of the children we minister to lives with both of his biological, married parents. In just a generation or so, our society has degenerated from one in which most families are intact to one in which marriage is optional, children float from one home and parent to the next, and a complete, functioning family is a rarity.

How did we get here? How did a society change so markedly in less than a century? We can blame it partly on marriages in which the partners stayed together but didn't get along. We should realize that the Christian model of marriage has not been upheld and sanctified by believers in our age as it should have been. But we also need to realize that the left has had a plan in place for many decades, and the changes we see in our society today are going according to this plan. Allow me to quote from an articled called "The Overhauling of Straight America," published in *Guide Magazine* in 1987. "At least in the beginning, we are seeking public desensitization and nothing more."[1] Members of the gay community began their infiltration into polite society by introducing gay characters in TV shows like *Barney Miller* and *The Odd Couple*. These men were portrayed in a comedic way—as odd individuals in a world that didn't understand or respect them. After repeated mentions of any topic, the shock value diminishes—so after people were no longer shocked by alternative lifestyles, the characters portrayed in TV and elsewhere became more mainstream and accepted.

The next goal of the gay movement was to soften the criticism of churches against homosexuality.

> This means publicizing support for gays by more moderate churches....
> Second, we can undermine the moral authority of homophobic
> churches by portraying them as antiquated backwaters. ... [2]

This is exactly what has happened. We as a society have come to look on alternate sexual options as within the realm of normal. Psychological textbooks have removed gender dysphoria from their lists of disorders. Denominations have debated whether to perform gay marriages in their establishments, and some even ordain gay ministers. The foundational doctrines of Genesis, that God created the world and created male and female humans to inhabit it, has been rejected from modern society.

A few years ago I took part in a peaceful rally for parental rights. The rally was well advertised, both on Facebook and in other media. I expected that there would be those of other lifestyles showing up at our rally to cause trouble—and my suspicions proved correct. Our rally was scheduled to start at 2:00. When our family showed up just before noon, we noticed around 150 angry people waving rainbow flags with sayings like "Binary Schminary" emblazoned on them. They were having a counter-rally, and after their scheduled activity ended, they showed up at our rally to shout out catcalls and chants as the speakers tried to speak or to pray.

This is the kind of opposition one expects these days when one protests the degradation of our society. Name-calling and interruptions are the order of the day, not just for two groups representing opposite viewpoints on the grounds of the legislature, but also, regrettably, in churches and other Christian organizations.

Why bring modern political issues into a book about music? Well, this plan of attack outlined in 1987 is paralleled by the infiltration of rock music, not only into our society in general, but also into our conservative evangelical churches. Millenia ago, Plato wrote, "The ways of poetry and music are not changed anywhere without change in the most important laws of the city."[3] It is no coincidence that societal norms and laws have changed drastically in the decades following the normalization of rock music. The first step in transforming the music of an orderly society into the blaring sounds of disharmony and sensual rhythms heard today is desensitization. Through the media of movies and television, characters were introduced who played music with a new sound. As more and more of these strange sounds were introduced to our ears in our own homes, the strangeness of it dissolved into a sort of normalcy. What once was violently sensual and rebellious to the ears of the populace became a mere annoyance. When parents expressed suspicions and fears about the impact of these sounds on the souls of their children, they were labelled old-fashioned—laughed at by the children they'd been given to raise. The generation which first adopted rock music became parents themselves, and when their children chose even more raucous music than they themselves had enjoyed, they rationalized it as being just the new generation's taste in music. Occasionally the teenagers were told to turn the music down, but in general, over the decades, the objections became fewer and the acceptance of this new music became greater. And now? Just as those who disagree with sexual practices other than heterosexual monogamy are labelled homophobes, those who believe there is something morally wrong with the music of this age are called old-fashioned, out of step, legalistic, and worse. What in past was normal and beautiful in family structure as well as in music is now judged harshly by those who push the new morality or modern music. The methodology is the same, though the issues are different.

The way we experience music has changed greatly over the centuries. In Bach's time, a composer was hired to write music for his employer. That employer might be the church in a certain city, the city council, or a political ruler. Sometimes there would be public concerts; occasionally someone would travel from another city to hear the music of a composer they'd heard about through the grapevine. Most music that the common people heard was that played by families as they got together in the evenings—folk music that had been passed down for centuries.

And then came radio. With the advent of radio in the 1920's, people could hear music of all types right in their homes. No longer did they need to pull out the fiddle or go to a concert to hear music. It was easier just to turn the knob on the radio in their kitchen or living room. And it was here that the music of the common people began to make its most dramatic changes. The practice of folk music was neglected, and people began to listen to music and other programs on the radio with increasing frequency. Popular music was born. The opportunity to change the world through the new mass media of radio was not lost on the crafters of the new society. As people became more dependent on the radio for news and entertainment, new music began to be heard over the air waves. Music that strained the sensibilities of the adults became a tantalizing influence in the lives of its younger listeners. They thrilled at the new, sensual sounds.

With developments in transportation in the 20th century, thousands were able to attend concerts where they worked themselves into frenzies, swaying as the music encouraged their bodies to move in new and exciting ways. Rebellion became cool, and as rock music became old news, the culture shifted more and more into an atmosphere of sexual experimentation, drug use, immodest clothing, and family disintegration.

Dress styles change. There is nothing inherently good or evil about the changing of fashion. One may be godly whether one wears black, white, or fuchsia, and one's morals do not change when one puts on ruffles or a tailored suit. But as hemlines have shortened, necklines have dropped, and clothes have become both more form-fitting and transparent, more than just the cut of fabric or the type of material has changed—our morals have been affected by the changing styles. To some in the church, the biblical concept of modesty has become less important than the desire to fit in. We have, in some instances, left behind our decency in order to match the cultural norms of our times.

Other parts of our culture have changed, as well. We eat different foods than our grandparents ate. My forebears came from Wales. A typical meal for them was a cut of beef or pork, with potatoes they grew in their own garden, bread made from wheat grown on their farm, garden vegetables of turnip, parsnips, or peas, and tomato juice squeezed from their own tomatoes. This would be followed by stewed prunes, or perhaps, if the grandchildren were visiting, they would have the special treat of freshly made Welsh cakes, sweet and hot from the frying pan.

Today's family is more likely to heat up a boxed pizza, or order from the drive-through at McDonald's. Home-cooked meals are rare now, but if we do cook, we're more likely to try our hand at reproducing the latest ethnic food shown on our favourite cooking show or found on one of the many recipe sites on the internet.

Technology has changed. My great-grandparents used horses to plow their fields. In later life, when their sons began farming on their own, tractors took the place of the work horses which had pulled the farm equipment. In my father's time, the automatic transmission and the ball point pen were invented. When I was in high school, my school library purchased the first school computer I'd ever seen. I got my teaching degree and began to teach school in rural settings where the electronic typewriter was the latest technological fad. Today, not only does almost every North American family have at least one home computer, but our lives are ruled by such devices as cell phones, GPS's, and autonomous cars. What changes in technology our generation has seen!

Some of the changes that have come about in the last century have been introduced to our society from cultures in other lands. During the First and Second World Wars, North American soldiers saw Europe, Asia, and Africa. They met the people there and were exposed to the music, dress, food, and culture of those places. They brought home Japanese kimonos, Chinese food, pizza, and an interest or belief in the false religions of the places they had visited while in the armed services. The North American continent, which had been populated largely by Anglo Saxons, the French, Eastern Europeans, Indigenous peoples, and a few Asians at the beginning of the twentieth century, became home to immigrants from Vietnam, Hong Kong, Taiwan, Somalia, Ethiopia, Kenya, Italy, and Mexico.

Along with all of these other changes to our society, the public's attitude towards the Bible has changed. Observe the following account of the significance of the Scriptures in communicating truth during the Second World War. This story is told by Dr. Robert B. Sloan, president of Houston Baptist University.

> Up until the 20th century, nearly the entire English-speaking world used the King James translation of the Bible. We all shared a common text. People were also more Biblically literate than most are today, so if you quoted a Bible verse people would usually recognize the reference. Bible stories like those in the book of Daniel were very familiar.
>
> In the summer of 1940, more than 350,000 soldiers—most of them British—were trapped at Dunkirk. The German forces were on their way, and they had the capacity to wipe out the British Expeditionary Force. When it seemed certain that the allied forces at Dunkirk were about to be massacred, a British naval officer cabled just three words back to London: 'But if not.'
>
> 'But if not.' These words were instantly recognizable to the people who were accustomed to hearing the scriptures read in church. They knew the story told in the book of Daniel.[4]

Daniel and his three friends, Hananiah, Mishael, and Azariah, had been captured in the land of Israel and taken to Babylon, where they eventually became government officials. When they refused to be involved in idol worship, the king ordered them to be thrown into a furnace. They replied that the God they served was able to deliver them from the fiery furnace—But if not, be it known unto thee, O King, that we will not serve thy gods. (Daniel 3:18) They were stating that they hoped that God would rescue them—but that even if He did not, they would rather die than worship false gods. The soldiers in WWII were stating a similar thing—that they trusted in God to deliver them from the Nazis—but if not—if they perished in the attempt—they would rather die trying than to give up fighting the evils of the Third Reich.

Those three little words, told and retold among the common people of England, led to the largest civilian-led military evacuation in history.

Fishermen, owners of leisure boats, and merchant marines convened on the coast of Dunkirk and rescued those brave defenders of liberty. Well over 300,000 soldiers were taken to safety across the British Channel.

These three words, "But if not," would mean nothing to the average man on the street today. There is no way we could portray the urgent need of soldiers in similar circumstances in just three words. Biblical literacy has fallen by the wayside in our modern generation.

In 1968, when astronauts Jim Lovell, Bill Anders, and Frank Borman became the first humans to orbit the moon, the event was televised. Because of the intense popularity of the space race at the time, an estimated one billion people watched the live broadcast. The astronauts had been asked to provide a reading that would be heard by earth's inhabitants while they traversed the heavenly realms. Together they decided that Genesis chapter 1 would be the ideal reading. They took turns reading the verses together, describing how God is the Creator of the earth and of everything in the heavens—giving glory to their Creator.

> Even 45 years ago there were atheist malcontents poised to complain about such demonstrations of good will. They were led by the founding mother of militant American secularism, Madalyn Murray O'Hair, who collected some 28,000 signatures on a lawsuit petition demanding that astronauts—or any other government employee—be prohibited from citing Scripture while on duty. In response Americans sent NASA more than 2.5 million letters and petitions in support of the Apollo 8 astronauts' actions—and O'Hair's lawsuit was ultimately dismissed by the Supreme Court.
>
> In the years ahead the U.S. Postal Service issued a six-cent postage stamp that featured the Earthrise photo along with the words, In the Beginning, in honor of the three astronauts and the day in history when they acknowledged God to the watching Earth.[5]

In a later flight to the moon, astronaut Buzz Aldrin partook of the elements of communion.

Fast forward to today. Not only would Scripture not be allowed in a broadcast from space, but it's not to be read publicly in our schools. Politicians avoid mentioning their faith for fear of losing points in the polls. If a remote Scripture were publicly quoted today, as it was in 1940 on the beaches of Dunkirk, it would go right over most people's heads. The Bible is commonly ridiculed and misquoted in public discourse, and Christians are seen to be narrow-minded, unintelligent nitwits who can't separate fact from fancy.

The beliefs of the people groups of the world are reflected in their cultures. These beliefs impact their view of scientific principles and help or hinder their scientific progress. Tribes which are involved in animistic beliefs tend to be very primitive, with little in the way of modern scientific development or fine art. In contrast, some cultures have made huge technological advancements: the West, Israel, and China, for instance. China's history includes much belief in our Creator, as is evidenced in the pictographs they still use.[6] Israel, of course, has been the people through whom God has chosen to reach the world, from almost the beginning of time. And the West has been fully engulfed in Christian doctrine since the time of the Reformation. It is no coincidence that these cultures with a background of recognizing God's truth have been the home of great advances in technology.

Great strides have been made in the realm of science by Christians. Isaac Newton repeatedly claimed to have made his discoveries by studying God's truths. Mathew Maury discovered ocean currents by reading about the "paths of the sea" mentioned in Psalm 8:8. Rocket scientist Werner von Braun thought that the achievement of manned space flight gave man a wonderful opportunity to explore the creation of God, and should serve to confirm a belief in God.

Besides the scientific advances made by Christian scientists, much social reform has occurred in places where Christianity is the dominant religion. Christians have, through history, founded orphanages, hospitals, schools for underprivileged children, soup kitchens, and works to benefit mankind. Yet, these days, they are accused of holding back social progress, of being scientifically unenlightened, and of being a hindrance to society. It is apparent that many discoveries and developments were made because of the faith that certain individuals had in God—that God enlightened and inspired these people to make the discoveries they did—and that they could not have made these advances apart from their firm belief in God, and in God's Word as the source of all truth.

What do all these changes have to do with music and morality? Perhaps the preponderance of music that appeals to the flesh has influenced some to make decisions, based on fleshly desires rather than logical reasoning and objective truth. It should be no surprise that listening to ungodly music changes our world view. In the book *Questions and Answers of World History*, the following question is asked and answered:

> How did the spread of liberal ideas change the world?
>
> Ideas of liberal democracy spread around the world after World War II, partly as a result of the Allied victory in the war… during the 1960s, there were protest movements by some American and European university students against the involvement of the USA and European countries like France in the Vietnam War. The liberal ideas of these youth leaders gave rise to large-scale anti-war movements around the world. New forms of music pioneered by bands like the Beatles helped these ideas to spread, leading to a sense of rebellion against the establishment and traditional society. This had a far reaching impact in many countries—church attendance declined and age-old social institutions such as marriage lost some of their significance.[7]

This secular source states that the music of the Beatles and others helped to foment a sense of rebellion against the establishment and traditional society. The lyrics certainly did so, but it was more than that. It was the music the lyrics were paired to, which was written to appeal to the new youth culture. There had never before been a youth culture like this—mobs of teenagers gathered in concerts and other events. The new music they developed was the banner of their counter-cultural society.

Alexander Solzhenitsyn was asked to give the 1978 commencement address at Harvard University. During his speech he said, "There are meaningful warnings which history gives a threatened or perishing society. Such are, for instance, the decadence of art, or a lack of great statesmen." We see these warnings in our society. Google defines decadence as "moral or cultural decline as characterized by excessive indulgence in pleasure or luxury." We are excessively indulgent. Children are raised to adulthood having never put in a day's labour. They are unaware of where food comes from. They've never grown a garden or raised meat animals. Art has degraded from being orderly and beautiful to being full of abstractions and crude objects. Music has gone from something which can lift one's soul in beauty to the coarse, raking voices and guttural noises produced by some of today's artists. And need we speak of the lack of great statesmen?

So, our culture has slipped. Our legislation and mores are no longer formed by the principles of God's Word to the extent that they were in the past. This departure from truth, beauty, and righteousness is seen in the art that is commonly found in galleries: we have gone from the beautiful realism of the early 18th century to today's dark abstractions with indiscernible objects and meanings. Clothing has become much less discreet, and the graphic designs found on the T-shirts of our youth display skulls, claw marks, vampires, and lewd sayings. Modesty is, fashion-wise, a thing of the past. God's Word has been removed from the schools, and has been replaced by some children being forced to repeat Muslim prayers and learn revisionist history.

How far we have slipped! We have left belief in God in the dust, as a culture, and whatever benefits we still enjoy from being a country with its moral tenets based in God's Word are enjoyed apart from any belief in God, as far as many are concerned. Great changes have come about in our society. I believe that a large catalyst for that change has been the degradation of music.

> As individuals turn further and further from the personal, infinite God, the Giver of gifts, *the more dehumanized and twisted will be that which he or she creates* ... There is the lostness of man, but ultimately the Christian should be hopeful and not write music that is harmful in this fallen world.[8] (Italics mine.)

CHAPTER 8

Changes in the Church and in its Music

The cultural shift in the North American church in the twentieth and twenty-first centuries has been nothing short of earth-shaking. We, as a church, have almost mirrored the cultural changes of the world around us, muting our distinctiveness as a set-apart group of believers who sought to be holy and to lovingly present the gospel, and trading that for an identity which makes it hard to tell the average Christian from a non-believer.

At the turn of the twentieth century in North America, it was the norm, culturally, to go to church on Sunday. Stores were closed, and businesses shut down on the Lord's Day. Women wore dresses and hats to church. Swearing was considered very crass, and only the lowest of the low used the Lord's name in vain. And yet now, well into the 21st century, we hear God's name used as a swear word every hour on TV, in almost every movie, even those rated G, and in the mouths of adults and children alike. For the last twenty years or so, it has not been highly unusual for even those who call themselves Christians to use God's name as a swear word.

Until the late twentieth century, most weddings were performed in church, funerals were conducted in the churchyard, and the minister was a well-respected member of society. Today almost anyone who holds to a Christian faith is ridiculed in the media and held suspect as potentially being mentally deficient at best, or a predatory pervert at worst. Many couples never bother with matrimony, and if they do, the ceremony could be held in a park, in the air while sky diving, in someone's home—but we no longer assume that weddings are held in a church or that the ceremony will ever make mention of God. Funerals are held in funeral homes and often the speaker has no sure hope to offer those who grieve. Ministers of the faith are ridiculed on prime time TV and are accused of all sorts of scandals—and some of them are found guilty of anything from adultery to embezzlement.

What changes our culture has seen! There have surely been some improvements: the development of antibiotics, cancer treatments, and life-saving surgeries. Foods from far-flung countries tantalize our palates. Fabrics, clothing, and decorations from various cultures colour our lives with their beauty. And yet, along with experiencing the delights of our shrinking globe come the dark parts—the pieces of culture that belong to Satan and false religion have taken firm root in our society. We are pressured to accept all lifestyle choices as valid, and many Christians have replaced the teaching of holiness with the doctrine of tolerance.

Have we lost all discernment? Can we not have the beneficial parts of each culture without the virulently non-Christian parts of them? Can we not keep ourselves from the evil that parades in our streets and woos us in our churches? For it has, indeed, crept into our churches. Many people who claim to be Christians have decided that God didn't really mean it when he stated that marriage was between one man and one woman for life. We break the speed limit, cheat on our taxes, swear at our spouses, and dress our children in sensual fashions; and then we have the nerve to call ourselves followers of Christ.

It doesn't take much digging to find that many of the practices introduced to the North American church in the last century have pagan roots. To some extent, various conservative Christians avoid those things; when they do, they stand out as different, weird, hung-up, stodgy Christians who are out of step with the real world.

The Bible doesn't give specific directions as to what to do and what not to do in every culture in every time period. Can you imagine what a huge book it would be if that were the case? Instead, the God of the universe has given us principles by which to live our lives as we navigate this world. He expects us to exercise our senses so that we will be able to discern between good and evil (Hebrews 5:14). Exercising our senses takes practice. We need to learn to discern. We're not always going to get it right. We're not always going to agree, even with other conservative Christians, but we must all make a strenuous effort to discern between good and evil.

What did Jesus have to say about the issue of holiness? He told us that unless our righteousness exceeded that of the scribes and Pharisees, we were in no way fit for the kingdom of heaven. He meant that we needed His righteousness, and there is not one of us who does not desperately need His redeeming work in our lives.

What is our response to this call to holiness, in the 21st century church? Many Christians see that it is impossible to be holy, so they give up the fight and choose to believe instead that they are pretty good—and that God will understand. But the Bible says in Titus 2:11–12, "For the **grace** of God that bringeth salvation hath appeared to all men, teaching us that, **denying ungodliness and worldly lusts,** we should live soberly, **righteously, and godly,** in this present world …" (emphasis mine). That is not what the cheap grace of today's church does. That grace tells sinners that Jesus loves them just as they are and desires no change from them. But in truth, the God of the Bible is holy, and He commands us to be so also. We are to be transformed by the renewing of our minds. (Romans 12:2) Of course, while we are in this world, we will never totally be sinless or completely holy, no matter how spiritual we are or how hard we try. Paul tells us in Hebrews 12:4, "Ye have not yet resisted unto blood, striving against sin." He's encouraging his readers to keep up the fight—to not lose heart in our struggle against sin. We are to continue striving for the holiness that is God's goal for us.

The more conservative members of the evangelical church still hold to the basic tenets of Scripture. They believe that Scripture is true, that God is good, and that Christ is our Saviour. But the discernment we need to fulfill God's command to "Be holy, as I am holy," seems to be in short supply in the church at large. We waffle in areas concerning Christian morals, and when it comes to music, the common belief is that as long as the words are okay, the music doesn't matter. And yet worldly music has had a huge impact in the radical alteration of the entire church atmosphere today.

Thirty-nine years ago, when I first became a Christian, many churches used only hymns in their services. It was typical to hear songs like "Amazing Grace." This song has been a classic for centuries. I'll print the first verse here. The syllables that are in bold are those that would normally be stressed if you were reading these words naturally.

> A**ma**zing **grace**, how **sweet** the **sound**
> That **saved** a **wretch** like **me**!
> I **once** was **lost**, but **now** am **found**.
> Was **blind**, but **now** I **see**.[1]

You can see that this verse reads like a poem: It flows well, and the meaning of the lyrics is clearly communicated because the natural stresses are reflected in the music. Every syllable of this hymn starts on a beat. This may not seem significant to you until you start to realize that very few words in many of today's church songs are started on a beat—any beat. The words that are in bold above are the ones that are placed on beat one of the music. Amazing Grace is written in 3/4 time, and the words in bold all fall on beat one—the strongest of the beats. The words were placed on this strong beat in order to emphasize their importance. Saved is more important than that, and so it is placed on the strong beat. Blind is more important than was, and so it also is placed on the more emphasized beat one.

In *The Screwtape Letters*, a book by C.S. Lewis which depicts a conversation in which an old, experienced demon teaches a young demon how to seduce Christians, the old one mentions to the young demon that he must instill in Christians a "horror of the same old thing."[2] Today's music leaders are always on the lookout for new music, and strongly shun the same old thing—hymns and other conservative Christian music—in favour of something new and different.

A couple of years ago, our family attended a Christmas service at a local church. We were expecting Christmas carols, perhaps a Christmas pageant, and a sermon on the nativity. Were we ever wrong! Only the first hymn sung was a Christmas carol. The lyrics, as is the case in most churches these days, were projected onto a screen at the front. The backdrop for the words was, for one song, the form of a woman in a yoga pose. After prayer, the congregation sang together "Jesus, Messiah." While the words of this song are actually very theologically sound, the rhythms are sensual.

The copyright laws concerning the use of song lyrics are very strict and can be firmly enforced. Therefore, I am unable to reproduce here the lyrics of various current songs and show you how they use stress in music. Instead, you can look the songs up on YouTube and try to follow along with the comments I make about them here.

In the song Jesus, Messiah, the stresses are not arranged in a logical fashion such as they are in Amazing Grace. Instead, the stresses fall haphazardly throughout the music. If you listen to the song, tap your foot in time to the beat and try to identify which words are given places of importance by being placed on a stressed beat. The strongest beats in this music are placed randomly throughout the song, occasionally happening on important words. As we have discussed previously, the strongest beat in any music is beat one. Interestingly, there is no word in the chorus of Jesus, Messiah that happens on beat one. Even though the words themselves mention Jesus the Messiah, none of the words is given the place of importance on the first beat. What is this communicating? Is it de-emphasizing the importance of Jesus as the Messiah, while purporting itself to be a song glorifying Him as Messiah? I don't think this was the intent of the writer of this song, but I do think that this is a subliminal effect of the music.

But what does it matter? Why would the placing of the stress within a song make any difference to the morality of the music? The next time this song is played in your church, take a look at how the people react. Typically, they will raise their hands and sway their hips. Spiritually uplifting music should not make one move in a sensual manner. The body and the spirit are inextricably linked for all of one's life. What affects the body can also affect the spirit, and if we willingly involve ourselves in music or activities that have sensual effects on our bodies, our spirits will definitely be affected too. When music, which is spiritually discerned, enters the body through the ear, it will often show its spiritual effect by movement. Sensual music will elicit swaying of the hips and other movements which we would also be likely to see if we were to look into a lounge where there was alcohol, music, and dancing. March type music will typically cause one to tap one's foot or nod one's head. Rousing music might cause one to clap one's hands or stomp one's feet—but only sensual music will naturally cause one to gyrate one's hips and move in a sensual manner. Therefore, when music in the church causes the congregants to act carnally, we ought to suspect that the music is not godly. Syncopated music typically brings out this sensual type of response from its listeners. Even if you yourself don't typically move like that when you hear these songs, if you can see that it has that effect on others, you would be wise and discerning to take note of that. Avoid youthful lusts, as says II Timothy 2:22.

Another song in the Christmas program we attended was *How Great is Our God*. Again, great words! But they've been put to music in a way that brings out the sensuality of the listeners. The words are placed on and around the beats of the music in an absurd manner. The word "the" is given more stress than the word "God." In this song, which has really wonderful lyrics, the emphasis is placed on words like "the," "in," and "to," rather than consistently placing due emphasis on the words "King" and "God." If one were to stress the important words in this song and reduce the syncopation, the result would be a song that was much more dignified and reverent. God is given His due glory when we speak His name in reverence.

God calls us to holiness—but what, indeed, is holiness?

In Exodus 15, when Moses and the children of Israel were singing a victory song after God rescued them from the Egyptians, they sang, Who is like thee, glorious in holiness, fearful in praises, doing wonders? In I Chronicles 16, David encouraged those who listened to his psalm to Give unto the LORD the glory due unto His name: bring an offering, and come before Him: worship the LORD in the beauty of holiness. Fear before Him, all the earth … In II Chronicles 20, Jehoshaphat was going against the Ammonites and the Moabites in battle, and

> he appointed singers unto the LORD, and that should praise the beauty of holiness, as they went out before the army, and to say, Praise the LORD; for His mercy endureth for ever. And when they began to sing and to praise, the LORD set ambushments against

the children of Ammon, Moab, and Mount Seir, which were come against Judah; and they were smitten.

In II Chronicles 31, Hezekiah broke down the idols and groves in Judah and re-instituted the worship of Jehovah. In doing so, he set apart the priests, for in their set office they sanctified themselves in holiness. In Psalm 29, David told us to worship the LORD in the beauty of holiness. The voice of the LORD is upon the waters: the God of glory thundereth ... Psalm 30 says, Sing unto the LORD, O ye saints of His, and give thanks at the remembrance of His holiness. For His anger endureth but a moment; in His favour is life ... In Psalm 47 we are told, Sing praises to God, sing praises: ... God sitteth upon the throne of His holiness. In these passages and more from the Old Testament, we see that holiness is very often mentioned in song. It is also evident that the holiness of God is very much related to His strength; notice how holiness is paired with a mention of His strength or a mention of the fear of God in most of these passages.

Holiness is cited in the New Testament as well. Continuing the Old Testament theme of God's holiness being linked to His strength in delivering His followers from their enemies, Zechariah mentions in Luke 1, That He would grant unto us, that we being delivered out of the hand of our enemies might serve Him without fear, in holiness and righteousness before Him. In the introduction to the letter to the Romans, Paul again connects God's holiness and His power: Jesus Christ our Lord, which was ... declared to be the Son of God with power, according to the spirit of holiness, by the resurrection from the dead ... Most of the references to holiness in the Old Testament seem to be about God's holiness, but in the New Testament, Christians are exhorted to be holy, too. Paul continues in Romans 6,

> I speak after the manner of men because of the infirmity of your flesh: for as ye have yielded your members servants to uncleanness and to iniquity unto iniquity; even so now yield your members servants to righteousness unto holiness. For when ye were the servants of sin, ye were free from righteousness. What fruit had ye then in those things whereof ye are now ashamed? for the end of those things is

death. But now being made free from sin, and become servants to God, ye have your fruit unto holiness, and the end everlasting life.

Paul repeats this theme in II Corinthians 7. Having therefore these promises, dearly beloved, let us cleanse ourselves from all filthiness of the flesh and spirit, perfecting holiness in the fear of God. He continues in Ephesians 4,

> If so be that ye have heard Him, and have been taught by Him, as the truth is in Jesus: that ye put off concerning the former conversation the old man, which is corrupt according to the deceitful lusts; and be renewed in the spirit of your mind; and that ye put on the new man, which after God is created in righteousness and true holiness.

Later in this same passage, Paul exhorts the believers to not let moral uncleanness or filthiness ever be named among them, and to have no fellowship with the unfruitful works of darkness ... (Ephesians 5:11). I Thessalonians 4:7 tells us God hath not called us unto uncleanness, but unto holiness. And in Hebrews 12 we are told to Follow peace with all men, and holiness, without which no man shall see the Lord ... Later in that chapter we're reminded that Esau traded something important (his birthright) for something that temporarily satisfied his earthly cravings (stew). Have we believers traded something holy for that which satisfies our earthly cravings? Instead of putting off the deceitful lusts of worldly music, have we clung to it and brought it into the churches? Have we cast aside the hymns and other godly music of old, and scorned the good hymns and spiritual songs being produced today, because we prefer that which is different and cutting-edge? The Old Testament links God's holiness to His strength. Perhaps one of the reasons the North American church lacks strength is because we have neglected the holiness that God has called us to in music and in life.

In church services today it is rare to hear prayers petitioning God for holiness or increased obedience to His Word. Instead, prayer focusses on increased love and passion, and the desire to hear God through prayer. Now, we do need to have increased love for our neighbours. You could say we need a passion for the gospel, a passion for holiness. We do need to hear from God through prayer. But it is easy to deceive ourselves into thinking that we've heard God say something through prayer that is actually contrary to what He has written in His Word. The tenor of our prayers often matches that of our singing: there is an emphasis on feelings rather than on truth and holiness. The music we use in church should not smack of the world and its race after fleshly living. Instead, the music we use to worship God should be characterized by holiness. May the church of God reject the fleshliness that plagues it, and instead seek God in holiness and humility.

CHAPTER 9

The Science of Music

It is both surprising and encouraging that so many scientific studies and observations have been made about music. From the physiological changes that occur when listening to certain types of music to the measurable changes in the size of regions of the brains of musicians to the effects of different types of music on the behaviour of plants, animals, and people, there is an abundance of knowledge about the effects of music.

Science is making great strides in understanding the brain, and as we progress in knowledge, we are seeing how very malleable our cerebral organ is. We know that there is a great amount of brain development which takes place in the infant and toddler years. There is also a substantial amount of development in the adolescent brain—and we have found that the male human brain continues to mature significantly until about age 25; female brains mature earlier. Recent discoveries in the world of neuroscience, though, have shown us that the human brain doesn't just stop developing at age ten, or twenty, or twenty-five. Although the early years are definitely times of great cognitive growth, the human brain has the ability to change and develop throughout life. The experiences we have continue to mold and shape our brains in ways we would never have imagined just decades ago. Our experiences in music can literally shape our brains.

Musicophilia is the title of a fascinating book written by a self-proclaimed "old Jewish atheist" named Oliver Sachs.[1] He was a psychiatrist who specialized in the effects of music on the brain and provided music therapy for patients with serious brain disorders. His book explains how music influences and forms the human brain. The author explains that the development of MRI technologies has enabled scientists to find and map the various changes made in the human brain when it experiences music.

> … [T]he corpus callosum, the great commissure that connects the two hemispheres of the brain, is enlarged in professional musicians and … a part of the auditory cortex, the planum temporale, has an asymmetric enlargement in musicians with absolute pitch.[2]

There are

> increased volumes of gray matter in motor, auditory, and visuospatial areas of the cortex, as well as in the cerebellum. Anatomists today would be hard put to identify the brain of a visual artist, a writer, or a mathematician—but they would recognize the brain of a professional musician without a moment's hesitation… the anatomical changes they observed with musician's brains were strongly correlated with the age at which musical training began and with the intensity of practice and rehearsal… the motor cortex can show changes within minutes of practicing … Measurements of regional blood flow in different parts of the brain, moreover, have shown increased activity in the basal ganglia and the cerebellum, as well as various areas of the cerebral cortex—not only with physical practice, but with mental practice alone… Takako Fujioka and her colleagues … have recorded striking changes in the left hemisphere of children who have had only a single year of violin training, compared to children with no training.[3]

Daniel J. Levitin, the author of another fascinating book called *This is Your Brain on Music: The Science of a Human Obsession*, tells us that musicians have

> larger cerebellums than nonmusicians, and an increased concentration of gray matter …[4]

These enlarged areas of the brain serve practical purposes. A study carried out in southern California examined young children who were involved in music lessons, a soccer program, or no special program. Using brain scans and other means of testing, the researchers found that the children who practiced music up to seven hours per week experienced accelerated brain development in the areas used for "language development, sound, reading skill and speech perception."[5] We can begin experiencing these positive changes almost as soon as we start practicing music.

> Even just a small exposure to music lessons as a child creates neural circuits for music processing that are enhanced and more efficient than for those who lack training.[6]

Researchers at the University of Vermont found that music lessons in childhood "provided tremendous benefits to children's emotional and behavioural maturation."[7]

The July 2003 edition of *Neuropsychology* showed that children who take music lessons for six years show an improvement in verbal memory. The longer one studies one's instrument, the better one's verbal memory becomes.

Being a music teacher myself, I have seen that most of my children are also musical and have been so since birth. Two of my children were born nearly tone deaf, but through much exposure to music and practicing of instruments, they have become, while not especially gifted in music, more capable of singing or playing an instrument in a manner that the listener can enjoy. It is apparent that it is both nature and nurture that develop the areas of our brains that deal with musical ability.

Not only does music affect the brains and behaviours of human beings, but it has an effect on plants and animals, as well. In 1973 Dorothy Retallack, a professional mezzo-soprano, preformed a series of experiments using music and plants. She used a variety of music in different chambers to see if it had any effect on the growth and health of the plants in those chambers. It's a fascinating set of experiments, and I encourage you to read it yourself.[8] To summarize her results, plants seemed to flourish when exposed to classical and North Indian music, but shrivelled and died when rock music was played. She wrote about this experiment in her book, *The Sound of Music and*

Plants. Plants have neither brains nor large internal organs, and no ears or auditory nerves. They are basically immobile, using sunlight, water, and soil minerals to create energy and the nutrients they need to survive. Humans are self-aware, thinking beings who dream and invent and travel—and hear. It seems odd to study the effect of music on plants and apply that knowledge to humans because humans and plants are so inherently different from each other. However, both plants and humans need air and water. Both groups react negatively to poisons. Both plants and humans are made up of cells, and both react to mechanical input (touch). So there are a few similarities, as well. If, as discussed in previous chapters, music has a spiritual component, it would then be possible for it to affect everything in the world: humans, animals, and even plants; simply because God, who is Spirit, has power over all things earthly. And we should also not rule out the possibility that Satan, who is also a spirit, can affect the physical realm.

The fact that any sound could have an effect on plants is fascinating, as we don't think of plants as being designed to process sound at all. But recent developments in the field of science demand that we re-think our under-standing of plants.

It is fairly well known that trees send their roots towards sources of water. How do they know where the water is? Dr. Monica Gagliano, a researcher at the University of Western Australia, has conducted a series of experi-ments with this question in mind. As explained in the May 2017 edition of *Oecologia*,[9] she found that not only did plants send their roots towards water pipes, even if those water pipes had no leaks whatsoever, but they also, incredibly enough, sent their roots towards a recording of flowing water placed outside the plant's pot! Somehow, those plants were responding to an auditory signal of the presence of water. Since we know that plants can respond to the sound of water, it seems less far-fetched now to realize that they do respond to music, as Dr. Retallack showed.

But whether or not we find it easy to believe that music has an effect on plants, it does have a measurable effect on animals. In 1997, a sixteen-year-old student in Virginia named David Merrill tested the effects of music on mice for a science fair experiment. He used three groups of mice in his study, giving each group the identical task of finding their way through a maze. The initial time for completion of the maze was ten minutes for each group of mice. Then David separated the groups of mice, and exposed one group to ten hours of hard rock music per day, and another group to ten hours of Mozart. The third group was the control group, with no music added to their experience. The control group, over time, decreased their maze-running time to five minutes. The mice listening to Mozart were able to complete the maze in only 2.5 minutes. But the group which was exposed to hard rock actually reverted in their learning, needing thirty minutes to complete the maze.

David had attempted this experiment at a previous time, but that trial was run slightly differently. In the first experiment, he allowed each group of mice to live together, separated from the other two groups. He found that in this earlier version of his experiment, the hard rock mice killed each other, while none of the other mice did so. Therefore, the second time he conducted this experiment, he was careful to keep all the mice isolated from each other.[10]

A similar experiment had also been conducted by two scientists in 1988: a neurologist named Dr. Schreckenberg and a physicist named Dr. Bird. Their objective was to determine whether there were any measurable changes in the brains of mice which were exposed to different types of music. They found that the mice which learned a maze while rock music was playing showed definite variations in the neuron structure of their brains. Some of these mice "resorted to cannibalism," and demonstrated "lethargy and inattentiveness." I encourage you to read the review of their study.[11]

Marianna Wertz, of the Schiller Institute, writes,

> ...Classical music is composed in coherence with what [Johannes] Kepler called the "harmony" of the universe, or the negentropic, creative mind of God, in whose image we are made. That it also has a salutary effect on such creatures as laboratory mice should not be surprising, since the same creative principles apply throughout all creation.
>
> The negative effect of hard rock or atonal music results from its purposeful rejection of that coherence, and its substitution of noise for harmony.[12]

A website called *Pracitica Poetica* discusses behaviour influenced by music. Carol and Louis Torres point out that our bodies use a complex orchestration of various rhythms. Our hearts, sleep patterns, brain waves and other systems all operate in complex arrangements. Rhythms found in music often mimic our own physiology. For instance, common musical tempos are played at the same rate as the typical human heart beats. Disturbances in this rhythm can result in changes in our bodies, increasing our heart rates and increasing the production of certain hormones. This change in physiological make-up changes our attitudes, emotions and manners in measurable ways.[13]

The power of music to align one's heartbeat and walking pace to the beat of the music is due to a phenomenon called automatic imitation. When a person sees or hears someone else doing a particular action, there are synapses in that person's brain that fire, encouraging the same response. This is the reason that your leg may kick a bit while watching an intense soccer game, or your gut may convulse when seeing someone punched in the stomach. Automatic imitation is thought to increase compassion in people. When we are walking in a shopping mall, and the sound system is blaring a song with a heavy beat, it's natural to walk in time to the music. It takes some concentration, actually, to walk to a different tempo.

The brain is an incredibly complex creation. It emits four different kinds of brain waves: alpha, beta, delta, and theta waves. Each of these waves induce different levels of alertness or relaxation. Our experiences and physical condition influence the production of the various types of waves. For instance, when falling asleep, our brains alter their wave patterns from beta to alpha, alpha to theta, and theta to the delta waves of deep sleep.

Music is another experience that affects our brain waves. When we listen to relaxing music, the brain produces more alpha waves, which help us to relax. The tempo of music has a measurable effect on our pulse rate and bodily actions. When we listen to music with a tempo at or just under our resting heart rate (50–70 bpm), our heart rate tends to slow, and we relax. Conversely, many rock songs are played at a tempo well over our natural heart rate (100–140 bpm). Listening to this music raises our heart rate and excites our impulses. When one adds to this fast-paced music lyrics that encourage rebellion or violence, one should not be surprised that riots are so common at rock concerts. The music has physiologically excited the listeners, so that they are inclined to be involved in screaming, rioting, vandalism, and the like. More about violence at rock concerts in Chapter 10.

In the late 1990s, the Berlin Senate financed a long-term study to observe the effects of classical music upon school children. They chose children from poor environments to be given lessons in singing or playing classical music, and found that after four years, the children who had studied this music were "more joyful, more intelligent, and more creative" than their counterparts.[14]

Andrew Pudewa, of the Institute for Excellence in Writing, has put together a quick fact sheet about the effects of music on plants, animals and humans which is worth perusing.[15]

The Mozart Effect became known in the early 1990's. It was observed that children who listened to Mozart's *Sonata for Two Pianos in D* performed better at tasks of spatial reasoning than did the control groups, who listened to relaxation tapes or silence. However, the effects of that music were only noticed for the ten to fifteen minutes following the study. Occasional, brief exposure to music makes only a small, short-lived effect to one's performance. Greater exposure to good music has a greater effect. Children who are exposed to classical music during the months before and after birth seem to have higher IQ scores than those without the same exposure. Children involved in choirs in which they study and perform classical music intensely do better at other academic pursuits than those without the same musical experiences.

> Since the mid-1990s, studies carried out by Robert Zatorre and his colleagues, using increasingly sophisticated brain-imaging techniques, have shown that imagining music can indeed activate the auditory cortex almost as strongly as listening to it. Imagining music also stimulates the motor cortex, and conversely, imagining the action of playing music stimulates the auditory cortex.[16]

Professor Nadine Gaab of Harvard Medical School has found that adults and children actively involved in music have higher executive function. She defines executive function as cognitive processes that include solving problems, setting goals, and thinking flexibly.[17]

Anne Blood of the Montreal Neurological Institute found in her studies in 1999 that music that brought out strong emotions in her research subjects stimulated areas of the brain normally associated with reward and motivation.[18]

When one has had a significant injury to one's brain in the area involved in emotional judgments, the parahippocampal cortex,[19] one may no longer be able to identify dissonance, the condition of notes being played together which produce a discordant sound.

Oliver Sachs describes people who have been struck by lightning, had a stroke, or for no discernible reason have suddenly developed an overwhelming, insistent interest in hearing and playing music. He mentions people with various psychological issues, and how they normalize when listening to music. Dr. Sachs tells of patients who experienced brain injury, and either lost or gained great amounts of musical interest *and ability* immediately following the traumatic event. After a stroke or other brain injury, those who normally enjoy music can develop different forms of amusia in which they can no longer recognize or enjoy one or more of the elements of music: rhythm, metre, melody, timbre, pitch, etc.[20] He tells of people born with mental challenges such as Williams syndrome, who are fascinated with music and sometimes excel at it despite their low IQs. Stroke patients may lose all ability to communicate in spoken words—but some of them can still sing, clearly enunciating all of the lyrics of songs they learned earlier in life. Some are not only able to sing along with these songs, but they are also able to converse coherently for some time after the music has stopped playing. Patients who, because of brain damage, lose the ability to read, may still be able to read music. Some may retain their ability to play an instrument but can no longer dress themselves.

In preparation for this chapter on music and science, I was overwhelmed by the amount of literature available that shows strongly that there is a definite effect made on the human brain by the amount and type of music it is exposed to. (More about the effect of different types of music in the next chapter.) I simply didn't have time to read the preponderance of articles, studies, and books which give solid evidence to the fact that the style of music we listen to makes a great difference in our brains and behaviour. I was actually quite surprised to find so much information. Over and over again, the convictions that God has brought me to about what music does to us have been confirmed and strengthened. My observations and conclusions have been repeated by scientists who have had the time and funding to study the problem, create experiments, and record the results. Much information has been discovered by scientists who are not Christians and have no apparent agenda regarding musical styles.

And yet there are plenty of people who have contended these results. In my reading of books and articles on the subject, and in my talking with people on both sides of the issue, the generalization I would make is that those who say that music affects us have carried out careful studies, documented their results, and speak with kindness, precision, and factual statements to show what they have learned. On the other hand, those who disagree that music effects us tend to resort to name-calling, insults and degradation to prove their point. That certainly doesn't apply to everyone I've talked to. Many people who will have an honest conversation with me about music have spoken politely, listened respectfully, and gone away with something to think about. On the other hand, there are those who have disagreed very strongly, without evidence to back up their claims. They have become vitriolic, spreading harmful lies about my husband and me because they disagreed with our stance on music. It's important that in this, as in all issues, we diligently seek the facts that will lead us to the truth.

Many proponents of rock, especially CCM, so devotedly defend their musical choices that they will not objectively consider evidence that their chosen form of music may be harmful, and musical styles which they do not appreciate may actually be good for them.

Objectivity is important when evaluating any moral choice. Music, however, is such an emotionally charged topic that it is extremely difficult to find someone who has no opinion about it and can be totally objective. Proverbs 16:16 tells us, "How much better is it to get wisdom than gold! and to get understanding rather to be chosen than silver!" It takes a lot of work to mine silver or gold, and we should expect that, in our search for truth, we will be required to work hard. The simple statements of our culture regarding the amorality of music cannot stand against the evidence, and we should dig until we find out the truth about the effect of music on the human brain.

CHAPTER 10
Music Affects Our Behaviour

As the saying goes, You are what you eat. This proverb condenses the thought that all that we are physically is made up of the elements we put into our bodies through our mouths. If we input junk food, we have little nutrition and lots of toxins and calories with which to run our bodies. If we eat healthy food, our body systems are nourished and tend to be healthy. Physically we are made up of our genetics and what we eat; emotionally, morally, and spiritually we are also influenced by what we take in. Debate has long raged over the question of whether the behaviour of children is influenced by what they see on television. Recent research has affirmed that yes, indeed, children's behaviour does change according to the visual and auditory stimulus that their TV viewing affords. Those who watch violence are more likely to become violent, and those who watch happy, innocent, playful shows are more likely to exhibit friendly behaviour.[1]

We know that music makes structural changes in the brain. It also enhances certain abilities. Exposure to music stimulates language proficiency, the development of compassion, and encourages motor coordination. Music also has an impact on behaviour—and we may notice that different kinds of music produce different effects on those who hear them.

Rock concerts are characterized by screaming fans, graffiti, and violence. Drugs and alcohol find their way into these events, and patrons become inebriated. It is not unheard of for someone to be trampled to death at a large rock concert. In contrast, a classical music concert is typically marked by order and decorum.

One might argue that violence is more likely to break out at an event with larger numbers of attendees, regardless of the reason for the gathering. Since rock concerts tend to have greater crowds in attendance than classical concerts, we might conclude that the number of concertgoers alone is the deciding factor in the levels of violence at an event. To consider this thought, we will examine the behaviours of people at large and small-scale events.

Classical performances typically attract fewer concertgoers than concerts of popular rock groups, but we may compare violence between classical concerts and small-to-medium sized rock music events. In April of 2010, there were several incidents of gunfire in nightclubs in Edmonton, Alberta, in which rock music was being played. After a number of violent incidents, one bar had restrictions placed on its license, and was later shut down.[2] It was a large night club, possibly serving several hundred patrons at a time. It's very likely that the presence of alcohol fueled the violence at the Iron Horse Pub, but alcohol was not the sole influencing factor, as rock and jazz music were played at that establishment, and we have seen that these forms of music can have negative effects on the behaviour of their listeners. A small classical concert would host about the same number of patrons, but it is difficult or impossible to find reports of violence at these small concerts. A performance at a symphonic music hall would hold a few thousand people, but again, violence is rarely or ever reported at such a venue.

The attendees at a large rock concert may number 18,000 to 20,000. A similar number of fans might be found at a professional sports event. Hockey games draw large crowds, similar in size to concerts held by such bands as Dixie Chicks or Deer Hunter. At a hockey game, some violence between players is expected. However, violence between fans at a hockey game is relatively rare. Considering the fact that there are thousands of fans cheering for two different teams at any hockey game, that's pretty remarkable. The rare altercation does occur: in March of 2016, there was a brawl that broke out between fans cheering for opposite teams in Unity, Saskatchewan. No lives were lost; no major injuries suffered. Hockey fans normally leave the stadium in an orderly manner and head home safely.

It used to be that people dressed up for a classical concert. Nowadays, you may find people in almost all manners of dress at the local symphony. The orchestra, however, still appears in their tuxes and black dresses. Concertgoers quietly sit in their seats, clapping at the correct times and leaving in an orderly fashion. No graffiti is seen on the walls of the concert halls, and no violence occurs as the concert ends.

No tuxes are seen at a rock concert. Jeans with holes, net stockings, and miniskirts are the attire of the attendees. Inebriating substances are consumed, wild screaming may ensue, and people are jostled during and after the concert. Injuries sometimes result, and graffiti is a common occurrence at and around venues which host rock concerts. Why the difference between the levels of crime and violence at the two types of concerts? Is it just that different people go to the different concerts? That can't be the only reason for the difference. Many people attend both rock and classical concerts. Is it the location that causes the increase in violence? A rock concert could be held at a sporting arena or a convention centre, and rock and jazz are played in most night clubs. We aren't likely to see violence after a baseball game or a trade fair, even though they may use the same venue as the rock concert. A church which moves into a building previously occupied by a night club typically has no problem with violence. Music halls designed for orchestras are often placed in city centres, close to locations where homelessness, drug use, prostitution, and crime occur regularly, and yet these concerts are very rarely the scene of violence. No, I assert that much of the difference in levels of violence comes largely because of the music itself. Rock and jazz music have power to change the heartbeat, to raise the blood pressure, to lower inhibitions, and to incite the spirits of their listeners to riot. Classical music does not normally do any of these things.

That violence at rock concerts is a fairly commonplace occurrence is a well-known fact among police officers. I spoke to an R.C.M.P. officer who confirmed my suspicion that, in his experience, there are frequently crimes committed during and after the concert of a rock star, but never or extremely rarely after a classical concert.

It takes very little web searching to find all kinds of violence that has happened at rock concerts. In 1952, Alan Freed organized a rock concert which ended in violence as the concertgoers ended up on the streets of Cleveland, Ohio, rioting and looting. On December 6, 1969, during the Altamont Free Concert, both concertgoers and performers were struck and stabbed, resulting in 4 deaths and 850 injuries in the crowd of 300,000. In a London, England concert performed by David Cassidy in 1974, nearly 800 people were injured in a stampede, and one teenage girl died of her injuries a few days later. This was certainly not the first time one of Cassidy's concerts had set off mass hysteria and riots. He was deported from Australia after one such concert. Cassidy, like other rock musicians, became an alcoholic.[3] In Donington Park, England, there was a Monsters of Rock event in 1988 that resulted in two of the 100,000 attendees being crushed to death while Guns N' Roses was playing. The same band was scheduled to play after Metallica at a concert in Montreal in 1992. Both groups had health issues which caused them to leave the stage prematurely. This led to a riot among concertgoers, in which a car was burned and dozens of small fires were started. In the 1999 Woodstock music festival, a woman who was crowd-surfing was gang raped. There were several other reports of rapes and sexual assaults during and after that event. Attendees ripped wood off the walls and security fence and used it for fuel. The grunge band Pearl Jam was playing at a Roskilde concert in 2000, when nine fans were crushed to death. On October 30, 2003, Marilyn Manson was playing for a crowd of 12,000. When the crowd broke down the security fence, not once, but twice, Manson left the stage. This led to 2000 crowd members damaging the property, throwing urine-filled bottles at police, and destroying cars. One man tried to run over a police officer. In the end, seven people were injured. In 2006, at a large concert in Georgia, the metal group Korn played while there was a scuffle resulting in the death of one of their patrons. A fan set fire to the stage where Bring Me the Horizon was performing in Sydney, Australia in 2013, and shot flares into the mosh pit, injuring concertgoers. On February 20, 2016, a struggle involving physical violence and taser guns erupted between fans and security officers at rapper Skate Maloley's concert in

New York. Two concertgoers were assaulted at a Phish concert in The Gorge in July of 2018. It's easy to find accounts of violence at rock and rap concerts— violence is a relatively expected part of that lifestyle.[4] There's even a folk/punk/ blues/jazz/rock band named Violent Femmes.

The relationship between any form of rock music and violence seems fairly clear, but those who like certain forms of rock defend it by saying that it doesn't produce as much violence as the other forms of rock. Karen Froeling writes that violence at a discotheque exceeds the violence of a rock concert.[5] Benjamin Welton tells us,

> To those not in the know, your average punk rock or hardcore show has the appearance of a riot, but the truth is that most mosh pits are controlled acts of violence, with unspoken rules dictating proper behavior. That said, real violence is not a rarity at punk shows. During the 1980s, when hardcore punk was being born, shows routinely turned violent as fans pounced on fans or, occasionally, tried to pick fights with the band members themselves.[6]

Whether there are controlled acts of violence or uncontrolled ones, and no matter how much violence is occurring, we ought to be concerned when any regular activity breeds repetitive acts of aggression and harm. Why do we continue to allow these events at which the very nature of the music encourages savagery?

Alcohol and drugs are often in use at rock concerts, and that could be a factor in the violence for which those events are known. Interestingly enough, however, patrons of classical music don't tend to bring intoxicating substances to their concerts. Having gone to scores, if not hundreds, of classical concerts, I've never seen anyone partaking of alcohol or drugs at these events, outside of the single glass of wine they may purchase during intermission. Rock music and alcohol somehow seem to belong together. The same could be said of jazz music, which is used in night clubs across the continent.

In 2007, the police in Colorado Springs blamed the rise in crime on the popularity of hip hop music. They believed that gansta rap and other music had lyrics that encouraged violence. In the article examining the topic, those who believe the music influenced the crime rate cite facts and numbers, while those who argue that the music did not cause the rise in crime simply complain about people wanting to stop hip hop.[7]

The behaviours brought about by rock music are not coincidental. The very purposes of rock music have been clearly stated by its proponents. Here are just a few quotes from professionals in the music field, stating the nature and purpose of their style of music.

Rock music is sex. The big beat matches the body's rhythms. Jimi Hendrix, *Life*, June 28, 1968. Notice he didn't mention anything about the lyrics.

"Rock 'n' roll is 99% sex." John Oats of Hall and Oats, *Cicus*, January 31, 1976.

"That's what rock is all about—sex with a 100 megaton bomb, the beat!" Gene Simmons of KISS, *Entertainment Tonight*, ABC, December 10, 1987.

"Rock 'n' roll is all sex. One hundred percent sex." Debbie Harry, *The Truth about Rock*, page 30.

"…the whole idea of rock 'n' roll is to offend your parents" King Coffey, *The Truth about Rock*, page 30.

"Listen, rock 'n' roll AIN'T CHURCH. It's nasty business." Lita Ford, *Los Angeles Times*, August 7, 1988.

When I taught in public and private schools, it became my observation that obedient children were smarter. Those who had been taught to obey as young children actually understood the concepts I was trying to teach them more quickly than those students who were in the habit of disobeying the authorities in their lives. That was at least partly because the obedient student was actually listening, whereas the disobedient student may not have been self-disciplined enough to do so. However, having observed this phenomenon on many occasions and in varied settings, I'm inclined to believe that obedient children actually are smarter. Perhaps, in God's infinite wisdom, he has ordered our lives so that when we follow His directives and obey parents and those in authority, He blesses us by ordering our brains in ways that are consistent with academic success. Meanwhile, those who reject God's order also reject the logical constraints and patterns of learning that lead to intelligent thought. Of course this is not a formula or a guarantee, but rather a general observation. There are many very intelligent atheists, and there are intelligent rebels.

I also noticed, while teaching in schools, that children who listened to rock music were inclined to be grumpy, inattentive and disobedient, while those with more conservative musical habits tended to be more cheerful and cooperative. This is a broad generalization, but it does hold some merit. Such an observation couldn't be made in most schools today, as the music of our culture has become much more saturated with rock and roll and its descendant musical forms than it was just a few short decades ago.

Just as the brains and behaviour of the mice in the University of Colorado experiment changed due to the music they were listening to, so humans change depending upon what type of music is on their playlists. A study in the *Journal of the American Academy of Child and Adolescent Psychiatry* examined different lifestyle choices between youth who preferred pop music and youth who preferred rock/metal music. Of course, most pop music is just a softer form of rock, but this study does show that the harder forms of rock are associated with more harmful behaviours in its listeners. The authors state that "Significant associations appear to exist between a preference for rock/metal and suicidal thoughts, acts of deliberate self-harm, 'depression,' 'delinquency,' drug taking, and family dysfunction." While more boys than girls preferred heavy rock and metal music, girls who like rock/metal music were even more likely to be engaged in these activities than boys of similar tastes. Youth who did not live with both parents were more likely to prefer rock/metal; again, this association was more pronounced in females. Twice as many rock/metal listeners as pop listeners reported that they were "not close" with their families—with females, this was three times as often. "More than 31% males and 66% females preferring rock/metal claimed suicidal thoughts in the previous 6 months compared with 14% and 35%, respectively, for pop."[8] Similar figures were true for incidents of self-harm in listeners to rock/metal. In this case, the incidence of self-harm for listeners to pop music was very low. The assumption of the writers of this study was that those adolescents with difficult lives gravitate to rock/metal music. I'm sure that's the case; but I also suggest that listening to rock music, particularly the darker forms of that music such as grunge, metal, and screamo, increases feelings of despair in its listeners.

There were previous studies, in 1988 and 1991, that also linked "disturbed or drug-abusing youngsters" with heavy metal music. The effects of continual involvement in rock music is also felt among its performers. For instance, Rapper Lil Peep died at age 21 of an apparent drug overdose in 2017. He was known for candidly talking about his depression, drug use, and bisexuality. People who are involved with this music are affected by it.

What are we doing to our kids?

We all know that music effects our emotions. In Hollywood, great care is taken to script just the right music for the movies which are produced there. The music makes a funny movie much funnier, a scary movie more terrifying, and a romantic scene more touching. Music aids in producing a feeling of suspense, of happy family times, of peaceful enjoyment of nature, or of gripping fear. The music in the movies intensifies our emotions in a way that the script and acting alone cannot. Music is powerful.

In Chapter 5, several verses were mentioned that encourage believers to sing to the Lord. By doing so, we are able to encourage ourselves and bring our emotions back in line with an attitude of gratefulness and joy. Our emotions are changed by the music we listen to—there really can be no disputing that. Rock music's raw power can change our emotions to encourage rebellion, licentiousness, hopelessness, and despair.

Screaming became popular at concerts in the early years of rock and roll. The fans screamed as their idols came on stage. The singers began to lend a screaming quality to their voice at times. Parents were aghast at the behaviour of the musicians—and of their children who were listening to this new music. For new music it was. The most basic tenets of traditional music were turned on their heads to become something quite different than the music of generations past. No longer did families gather together to play folk songs in the kitchen. Now the teenagers wanted to go to the concerts of famous singers, where they might scream and cry—where they might be introduced to drugs and alcohol—and where opportunities were given for unbridled sex. Obviously, parents were not welcome here.

Undue attention began to be focussed on musicians. Teenagers bought the records of their favourite artists and talked about those performers with their friends. They bought magazines featuring their musical idols and put up posters of them in their bedrooms. These musical stars became not just popular, but really idolized. It was as if they were several steps above regular people. Even today, fans follow Justin Bieber or other young singers, demanding a selfie with them, or an autograph, or wanting to kiss them. If this behaviour was carried out on other people—the average person you might find on the street or in a bus—we would think it highly irrational. And yet this idolatrous behaviour is commonplace in the music industry today. And it's not much better in the Christian music industry than it is in secular music. Christians, too, have their favourite bands or singers. They talk about these people with their friends, go to their concerts, and read about them in magazines. Adult Christians post pictures of themselves with their favourite singer on social media, and buy exorbitantly priced tickets to "Christian" rock concerts, even flying to different countries to experience first-hand the music of their favourite group.

In an interesting article on Wikipedia called "Social Effects of Rock Music," the author mentions that when drug use among rock musicians became known, it became more common for their followers to use drugs. Rock fans also copied the clothing that their favourite musicians wore.

How is this behaviour different from the way a person acts when he is an appreciator of good music? Discerning music lovers do not tend to lose emotional control over their favourite orchestra member. As a matter of fact, it seems rare for a discerning Christian to even *have* a favourite modern classical performer. They are unlikely to have fan posters up in their rooms. Their appreciation of a particular artist doesn't usually become an unhealthy obsession. A ticket to a concert with Five Finger Death Punch costs up to $333, while the highest priced ticket I could find to a local concert of music by Bach, Haydn and Schubert costs $59. The difference in price does not reflect the respective abilities of the musicians.

Daniel J. Levitin was part of a rock band in his young adult years. While discussing his entry into recording music, he mentioned casually that several of the members of his band had a habit of getting high between takes at the recording studio. Because Daniel was sober, he was treated to more of an education in the behind-the-scenes technology of music production. Later, he states that the band broke up due to repeated suicide attempts. It is a shame that it seems common for those who are heavily involved in rock music to also be involved in alcohol, drugs, orgies, depression, cutting, and suicide attempts. There does seem to be a strong link between the activity (rock music) and the results (harmful and addictive behaviours).[9] Later, Mr. Levitin states that "The number of sexual partners for rock stars can be hundreds of times what a normal male has…"[10]

Forsyth, Barnard, and McKeganey reported that, "On the basis of the evidence presented, a significant relationship was found between identification with rave music and life-time drug use."[11] The *Journal of Adolescent Research* states that,

> Adolescents who preferred hard rock or heavy metal music reported higher rates of reckless behavior, including driving while intoxicated, driving over 80 miles per hour, sex without contraception, sex with someone known only casually, drug use, shoplifting, and vandalism. Preferences for hard rock or heavy metal music were also associated with higher levels of sensation seeking, negative family relationships, and, among girls, low self-esteem.[12]

A study published in *Pediatrics* shows that children who listened to various forms of rock music from an early age (metal, hip-hop, trance, etc.) became more involved in delinquent activities than did their counterparts who listened to pop, classic, or jazz music.[13] A study by P. King in *Adolescent Medicine* suggests that significantly higher percentages of disturbed or drug-abusing youngsters prefer heavy metal music.[14]

I home educate my children. One subject I teach them in school is music. During their elementary years, I teach my children the basics of music in classroom lessons and on the piano. By the time they reach junior high school age, I ask them to choose another instrument to play. Being a band teacher, I experienced a bit of consternation when five of my children chose to play stringed instruments, instead of the woodwind, brass, and percussion instruments with which I am familiar! I've had to hire teachers to instruct these five children in their chosen instruments.

Three of my strings-playing children have each taken music lessons from a cellist who plays with our local orchestra. Their teacher is an interesting man.

We've seen him all dressed up in his tux in the concert hall, sometimes also wearing red socks, a plaid vest, or even a string of Christmas lights! We've also seen him in his natural attire at music lessons: shorts worn over top of pajama pants, and ratty sweatshirts. His family runs a market garden, raises several kinds of animals, and enjoys quiet country living. I find him a fascinating individual. His wit is as finely tuned as his violin. There have also been several other string teachers who have given my children lessons over the years.

I doubt that any of their string instructors have been firm believers in Christ. I dare say each of them has his character flaws and idiosyncrasies. However, I know of none of them who take drugs, have attempted suicide, or cut themselves. I'm not saying that those who make a practice of playing and teaching classical music will never be involved in these activities; I am simply saying that they don't have a reputation for being involved in them.

If we look back through the history of music, we find that, in the Baroque era, drugs and alcohol were not used by musicians, with the exception of the wine and beer common in Europe. As music progressed through the Classical, Romantic, and Twentieth-Century eras, there were composers who did take some forms of illicit drugs, particularly opium. When music ceased being a medium with which to honour God, and became something with which to entertain oneself and make a statement, the lifestyles of the composers deteriorated.

The classical performers of today don't seem to have any higher rate of drug use than the average citizen. Rock musicians, on the other hand, have been known from the beginning of the movement to be involved in "sex, drugs, and rock 'n' roll." There is definitely a great lifestyle difference between a typical rock star and a typical classical musician. Why?

I believe it's because of the music in which they immerse themselves. Classical music is known for its beauty and order; rock music is known for its discordant, loud noises and rebellious tone. The Bible says, "by their fruits ye shall know them," (Matthew 7:20) and "Be not deceived; God is not mocked: for whatsoever a man soweth, that shall he also reap." (Galatians 6:7) I believe the difference in lifestyles between the two groups of musicians is largely because of the music they play. Rock and jazz have, at their roots, music brought from pagan cultures to the West through the slave trade. Tribes in

Africa who worshipped false gods were immersed in a form of music which was produced in the worship of these deities. When the people of Africa were captured and ripped from their homes by those who made their living by trading in human beings, the slaves naturally brought that style of music to the New World with them. Here, it took root and evolved into forms of rock and jazz music.[15] These forms of music commonly produce the fruit of unbridled sensuality and drug and alcohol abuse. On the other hand, the Reformation was a root of great music, both within and without the church, and the fruit of that has been the creation of a culture which has held Christian morals dear for centuries.

Over the decades, popular music has evolved. The raunchy electric guitars of the '70's have become more civilized in sound. Modern popular music has split into two basic factions: the chicken stomping music stars of the '70's have brought forth punk, and then metal, and then screamo and rap. The easy-listening singers such as Anne Murray have given way to Celine Dion and Josh Groban. But through it all rings the same spirit of rebellion; exemplified, if you will, in the backwards stresses that make rock music what it is. Soft rock, after all, is still rock. Its effects may not be as obvious as the effects of screamo on its listeners, but both still change their hearers.

CHAPTER 11
What We Like

At the moment when sin entered into the world, Eve didn't rely on logic or knowledge as she made her infamous choice—so why should we expect the youth of today to think clearly when listening to popular Christian music? In the Garden of Eden, Eve allowed herself to be led by the devil's lies and by her own sensual desires She saw that the tree was good for food, and that it was pleasant to the eyes, and a tree to be desired to make one wise. (Genesis 3:6) Like Eve, people in the 21st century simply make choices based on what sounds good to them, or helps them to experience pleasurable sensations. As Bruce Waltke and Cathi Fredricks write in *Genesis: A Commentary*, Satan engaged Eve

> into what may appear as a sincere theological discussion, but he subverts obedience and distorts perspective by emphasizing God's prohibition, not his provision, reducing God's command to a question, doubting his sincerity, defaming his motives, and denying the truthfulness of this threat.[1]

When one suggests to a music lover that some of the music to which he listens is detrimental to his spiritual growth, one may expect that person to present quasi-spiritual arguments as to why the musical choices he *likes* are just fine with God. The rock enthusiast will state that God never forbids rock music, and that our stance against it is simply because of our taste. The refrain of the song, Why Should the Devil Have all the Good Music is sung again, deceptively calling music that is fleshly good, and relegating as worthless the centuries of good music produced by talented musicians through the ages, as well as godly music currently being written. Science supporting the claim that sensual music leads to sensual acts is rebuffed. Copious proofs are demanded to prove the point that music changes people, while no scientific proof is given to support their view, that music has no effect.

Church leaders, ministry leaders, friends, acquaintances, and strangers have often dismissed our beliefs about morality in music by referring to our musical convictions as mere preferences. Once, when our family members were the only patrons at a restaurant which was playing raunchy music, we asked the waitress if she'd be able to change the station. She took a look at us, determined our approximate ages, and said, "Okay, I'll put on the eighties rock station." Before we could protest, she spun around and went to change the dial. While eighties rock is different in style and timbre than modern pop music, she had totally missed the point. We didn't want our young children exposed to rock music at all. Instead of changing the radio station to one that played music written anywhere between the thirteenth and nineteenth centuries (that's 800 years of music!), or one playing today's beautiful music, she switched from the music of the current decade to that of only two decades previous (at the time)—which was still a form of rock. Our society's musical view and experience is extremely myopic.

As Christians, we are called to die to the flesh. We are called to put off the things of our former lives—our habits and tastes that lead to debauchery, or that show the direction of our lives to be anything other than the narrow road of faith. Some of the lifestyle choices that God tells us to put off include lying, anger, stealing, corrupt speech, bitterness, malice and slander. Are we to put these things off because we don't *like* them any more? No! We're to reject these behaviours from our lives because God has created us as new, spiritually alive beings, and as His children, we are to change our behaviour to be more like His. In short, putting off these sins of the flesh is a matter of obedience. Given the choice, we might still enjoy a little gossip session with a friend, or telling lies meant to impress others, or stealing things that we want.

Some might enjoy drinking alcohol, watching x-rated movies, driving cars at reckless speeds, or disobeying authorities. Whether we like these activities or not, God commands us to put them off because now we are to act as Christians should. *What we like* has nothing to do with the lifestyle choices God commands.

We cannot, as spiritual beings, live by our own desires. We can't make our decisions based only on what we'd like to do. When we consider the demands of our God, of our employers, or of our parents, we will find ourselves in trouble if we follow the dictates of our flesh instead of our commitment to doing what is right. Who wants to get up in the morning and go to a job he doesn't particularly enjoy? Who wants to avoid sugar and fatty foods in order to experience better health? Who wants to give up the old friends who only want to hang out in bars? If we do only those things we *want* to do, we will follow a lifestyle of permissiveness and sin, and we will be useless to God.

I don't drink. There are several reasons I don't drink alcohol, and those reasons are not the subject of this book. Before I became a Christian, I did drink. I have tasted beer, wine, rum, vodka, various liqueurs, and other mixed drinks. While I have no idea why anyone would willingly drink something as vile-tasting as beer, I have very much enjoyed the flavour of some liqueurs. If I were to live only by the rule of doing what I wanted to do, I would still find myself in the liquor store, buying drinks to serve my flesh. However, since I have chosen to follow Christ as my Lord and Master, I have put my desires under His sovereignty, and I choose to not drink alcohol of any flavour.

I grew up in the 70's—the era of melodic rock ballads. I came of age in the 80's. In 1981 I was saved, and not long after that, the Lord convicted me that my music listening habits must change. While large changes to my listening habits were made in short order in obedience to His call, I have noticed that my sensitivity to good and evil in music has become more refined in the ensuing decades, and also that as some qualities of music change with fashion, I must continue to develop the discernment I need to rule my choices in new music.

My husband and I began our courtship in 1984. Well I remember sitting in Dallas Pizza, gazing across the table at my winsome young man as the stereo played, "I Can't Fight This Feeling Any Longer." Another song we enjoyed was, "I Just Called to Say I Love You." While I still experience an attraction to these and other songs, largely because of the part they played in our courtship, I choose to avoid listening to them any longer. While the words might be fine and the melodies are catchy, the rhythms and beat patterns of these songs are not godly.

Over the years, we have gone to a variety of churches as visitors, as speakers, and in search of a church in which to raise our family. As a result, we have heard many "Christian" songs used as part of the worship service of the church. Some of those songs are really catchy. Some have melodies that I would call brain worms because of the way they stick in your head. Some songs have no appeal at all. At times we have chosen to remain silent while songs were sung to sensual music, and occasionally we have quietly left a church service at which particularly ungodly music was being presented. But in all these things, we have chosen to seek God in terms of the types of music He desires us to be involved in. I can't stay in a church service, singing songs I like, only because I *like* them. I can't leave every time a song I don't *like* is played. Our desires must not be the sole determining factor in our music choices! What we like does not automatically have a place in the worship of our God. However, our choice of a church, our presence in a particular church service or activity, and our participation in singing, should be determined how God's principles agree with our knowledge and observations of the various styles of music.

I like musical pieces from varying styles and musical periods. Although Bach is my favourite composer, there are composers I respect and whose music I value in all periods of music. There are hymns I enjoy and which draw me into a deep worship of God. There are hymns I find boring or unscriptural. There are contemporary songs that are meaningful, have very singable melodies, and which I sing and teach others to sing. And there are contemporary "Christian" songs that are not at all suitable in the worship of a holy God. The time period in which a piece of music was written is not the determiner of whether it is good or bad; nor is whether we *like* the music a reliable determiner of its moral value. Whatever we sing, especially when we are using songs in our approach to Jehovah, the determining factor must not be whether we *like* the music, but whether God Himself is pleased with the musical offering we are presenting to Him. Is it holy, or is it not? Is it sensual or is it pure? Does it appeal to our flesh, our sensual, earthly desires, or does it truly bring us closer to the Lord of life and godliness? These must be the questions we ask ourselves honestly as we choose the styles of music we will use in our homes and in our churches.

If we feed the flesh, we will reap fleshly rewards. How many times have I heard of yet another Christian from a church with worldly music in its services, who has fallen to sin—primarily sexual sin? How many Christian girls who become pregnant without the benefit of marriage, while living a lifestyle rife with sensual habits like CCM, does it take before we make the connection that ungodly listening habits lead to ungodly lifestyles? I am not saying that everyone who ever listens to CCM will fall to sexual sins. I am saying that many do, and I assert that if we feed the flesh, we will have more trouble with the flesh than we would if we fed it pure music, entertainment choices, thoughts, and habits. Some will believe themselves to be strong enough to resist the fleshly call of rock and syncopated music. They believe that they will be the Christian who can listen to whatever they want to without any ill effects. Proverbs 22:3–5 says,

A prudent man foreseeth the evil, and hideth himself: but the simple pass on, and are punished. By humility and the fear of the LORD are riches, and honour, and life. Thorns and snares are in the way of the froward: he that doth keep his soul shall be far from them.

It's not that the simple man didn't see the evil—he just didn't recognize it as evil, or didn't admit that it had any power over him. Perhaps he believed himself to be invincible. It takes a great deal of humility to admit that perhaps there's something we don't know about the effects of rock music, and that perhaps our listening habits need to be revised. He who keeps his soul stays away from the thorns and snares of life that hurt a Christian and keep him from effectiveness. None of us are strong enough to intentionally play with spiritually harmful things and not be harmed by them. And yet, many Christians still think they can avoid that result: that they will not be so gullible as to fall for the deceitfulness of sin as expressed in sensual music. They think they're strong enough to survive. They're not. In even thinking so, in not obeying the scriptural commands to avoid evil and flee youthful lusts, they are already sinning.

Because we now have generations who have grown up with different forms of rock music being popular and accepted forms of entertainment, adults in our society are as undiscerning as youth in regards to the consideration of morality in music. However, the youth in each generation seem to push the limits, seeking more and more overt sensuality in their new musical styles. Young people who have grown up with more conservative musical standards in their homes sometimes chafe at the restrictions which make them different than their peers. In avoiding the often-repeated commands in Proverbs to listen to their righteous parents, some Christian youth and young adults have rejected God's guidance in their lives.

Peer pressure and cultural experiences strongly influence the music we listen to, and the music we grow to like. Most of our youth, and indeed many adults as well, are under such constant pressure to fit in that they accept what their group is doing or listening to without question. Therefore, what the group wears is what they wear; what the group listens to is what they listen to.

God has designed us so that the music we listen to can actually change the hard-wiring of our brains, and it can cause hormones to be produced which transform music into an object of deep emotion, and even addiction.

Science has shown us that the music we listen to affects the production of chemicals in our brains. These chemicals can affect our moods, which can influence us to passionately adore certain types of music. This passion has nothing to do with whether the music is morally good or bad, nor does it have anything to do with the artistic quality of the music. It is actually a consequence of *exposure* to that type of music that brings about intense emotions in the listener. If we are addicted to music that is ungodly, it's going to be really difficult to choose spiritually better music. We are drawn to what we like, or love—the music that calls to our emotions and passions. In addition to these physiologically and emotionally based musical motivations, the strong desire to belong to a group means that teenagers will emphatically cling to the music of their group. Usually, the musical experiences of teenagers are narrow, and they have not had sufficient exposure to enough musical styles to be able to actually make a fully informed decision when choosing their favourite musical styles. But since they feel the need to identify with their friends, they defend their right to listen to the popular forms of music enjoyed by their peers. It happens to adults, too. Even adults who have previously adhered to conservative musical standards can be drawn into listening to CCM because it touches them deeply, or because they want to identify with the younger generation or avoid looking old-fashioned to their fellow church-goers. None of us are immune to the lust of the flesh.

We must, as Christians, be willing to give up that which sounds its siren call to us if, when viewed objectively, we find that this music is not what God would have us listening to. We must mortify the deeds of the flesh—and killing our own flesh is by no means painless. Christ calls us to "Come out from among them, and touch not the unclean thing, and I will receive you," 2 Corinthians 6:17. (Read the whole passage; it's very much applicable to a discussion on what type of music to listen to.) If we give up a certain form of music, it's possible that some friendships and associations may change, because to continue these involvements is to flirt with unhealthy desires and temptations. This is a time that we must put on our armour (Ephesians 6) and fight like warriors, spiritually speaking, to do the work of holiness that God has called us to. He will reward those who follow Him.

Daniel J. Levitin holds a Ph.D. in neuroscience. His book, *This is Your Brain on Music*, gives a very readable, fascinating explanation of science's understanding of the effects of music on the brain. Near the end of this brilliant masterpiece is a personal reflection not bound by the limits of science, which aptly expresses the effect of music on one's soul.

> To a certain extent, we surrender to music when we listen to it—we allow ourselves to trust the composers and musicians with a part of our hearts and our spirits; we let the music take us somewhere outside of ourselves. Many of us feel that great music connects us to something larger than our own existence, to other people, or to God… We might be understandably reluctant, then, to let down our guard, to drop our emotional defenses, for just anyone… We want to know that our vulnerability is not going to be exploited… When I listen to the music of a great composer I feel that I am, in some sense, becoming one with him, or letting a part of him inside

me. I also find this disturbing with popular music, because surely some of the purveyors of pop are crude, sexist, racist, or all three.

This sense of vulnerability and surrender is no more prevalent than with rock and popular music in the past forty years. This accounts for the fandom that surrounds popular musicians ... We allow them to control our emotions and even our politics—to lift us up, to bring us down, to comfort us, to inspire us...

It is unusual to let oneself become so vulnerable with a total stranger.[2]

Do you hear the pathos with which the author describes the vulnerability of listening to a composer's music? He worries that if he listens to the music of Wagner, he will develop the same ugly thoughts that Wagner had. He understands, better than many Christians do, apparently, that to listen to music is to become like its composer. To have on one's playlist music written and sung by men who view sex with strangers as a pleasant evening's occupation may increase one's sexual desires in inappropriate ways. To listen to rappers chanting about the latest murder they've committed decreases our respect for the sanctity of life. And listening to Christian words set to music that has been created to wear down our inhibitions and increase our sensuality will do just that: the words contradict the power of the music, but the music reaches right into our souls and overpowers the saintly words that accompany it. It is foolhardy to listen to sensual music and think that we are above its powers. "Can a man take fire in his bosom, and his clothes not be burned?" (Proverbs 6:27)

Of course people like rock music. It appeals to our sinful natures, and we like the sensations that it brings. But God calls us to something better than that. He asks us to make sure that all our activities, whether music, movies, work, hobbies, or language, are all pleasing to Him.

I beseech you therefore, brethren, by the mercies of God, that ye present your bodies a living sacrifice, holy, acceptable unto God, which is your reasonable service. And be not conformed to this world: but be ye transformed by the renewing of your mind, that ye may prove what is that good, and acceptable, and perfect, will of God. (Romans 12:1–2)

Let us present our music preferences before God, and be conformed, not to the world's standards, nor even to the worldly church's standards, but to the perfect will of God.

This is not about what we *like*. It's about what is godly and what is fleshly. If we fill ourselves with fleshly input, we will yield a fleshly result. God's desire is that we "put away the unclean thing" and seek holiness. Will you?

CHAPTER 12

The Seduction of the Western Church

Worship is a term that is misunderstood by many. The strong *association* of worship with music has led many to *equate* worship with music. But worship is so much more than just music! The English word worship came from the Old English *weorthscipe*—or worth-ship. It was an acknowledgment of the worth of someone. So, to worship God, we show forth His worth. We can do this in prayer, in edifying speech, in silent communion, or in music. Saints through the ages have sung of the Lord's worth in their psalms, hymns, and spiritual songs. Music is an important part of worship, to be sure, but it is not the only part of worship. These days we speak of someone being the worship leader. We mean the music leader. We speak of leading worship, or in other words, leading singing. When we are called to worship in a church service, what is meant is, Let's sing.

It's an interesting correlation. While music does not equal worship, it is an integral part, and when we change the music, we do change the worship. As we discussed in the chapters on music history, Baroque music was chiefly about God. Classical music was about man and nature. Romantic music focussed on human emotions. And things just got darker from there. Instead of nobly writing beautiful music in response to devastating things in his life, as Tchaikovsky did, today's musician is encouraged to write what he feels. So, if he's going through a dark time in his life, he will write dark music. While this may be a valid expression of his soul, it's not necessarily something he should dwell on, nor share with the general public. Dark movies may accurately portray a real aspect of life, but their effect is often to depress and discourage viewers, without bringing about any positive change. Dark music affects people similarly. And just as the focus of music has gone from the eternal to the temporal, and from the external to the internal experiences of man, music in church has followed the same directional change.

In today's Christian music, most of the music seems to be about the writer. God will be mentioned in some form—sometimes in such a way that we aren't really sure who the song is talking about. But the basis of the song is how God has blessed me, or how I feel about God, or even just about the bad day I had. Some examples are "Safe With You" by Skillet, "Read All About It" by The Newsboys, and almost anything by Tenth Avenue North.

In our grandparents' day, music in church meant hymns. Songwriters have continually added to our library of hymns over the ages, so that some songs in our hymn books are a millennium old, while others were written in the 21st century. Hymn lyrics are typically about the attributes of God: His love, justice, power, etc. It is rare for a hymn which is more than a hundred years old to focus on the emotions of the author of the hymn rather than on the person of the Creator.

I have often heard the statement that some hymn writers of previous centuries used barroom tunes as the music to which they set their hymns. The Practica Poetica website gives a great explanation of how the musical term "bar" became confused in some people's minds with a bar—a lounge which serves alcoholic beverages.[1] That whole website is worth your perusal, as it presents many interesting facts about music.

When parents of the 20th century spoke out against sensual, rebellious-sounding rock music, CCM artists like Larry Norman came out with songs like, Why Should the Devil Have All the Good Music? The assumption, madly clung to by thousands of young Christians, was that the music which had been attributed to the devil was actually good, and we should be using it as Christians, too. How did they come to this conclusion? Did they have access to scientific studies that showed the brain and behavioural changes that happen when the style of music listened to changes so vastly?

Did they ask their elders for their wisdom? Did they search the Scriptures for God's enlightenment on the topic? No. They went with what felt good to them—they were ruled by what they liked. Torrey Johnson, founder of Youth for Christ, wrote in 1971, The corruption in church music is a reflection of the instability even of today's Bible-believing churches. This is evil.[2] In the 1980's we saw conservative churches allowing their young people to form worship bands that performed rock music in churches. Familiarity with this music in society at large led to its acceptance in God's house. Lowell Hart explains, The roots of the 'new' Christian music go back more than 100 years to the barrooms and dance halls of New Orleans where jazz and rhythm and blues were born.[3]

It became normal for Christian youth to listen to CCM. The CCM industry grew. Kids who'd been brought up in church began to dislike the old hymns and wanted *their* music to be sung in church. Kind and gracious church leaders let them have their way, not really seeing the harm in it. Generally, a traditional church would start their foray into modern music by just introducing a few modern choruses into the youth meetings. Sooner or later one or two of them would end up in a Sunday morning church service. This was the era of setting Scripture to song—and who could argue with the Bible set to music? Much of the new music fashioned for churches really was good at this time, too—it didn't have a rock beat, it wasn't syncopated, it was melodic, and the words were God-centred. There was nothing wrong with much of it. But then the backbeat started on the guitars or pianos or synthesizers. It was only soft rock—people thought it not so bad—what harm could come of it? But as the church members became used to soft rock, drums were introduced, and the music, little by little, became more sensual, less scriptural, less God-focussed. The beat became more prominent, and eventually the words hardly said anything about God at all. Oh, but the people were enjoying it! You could tell by the way they swayed while crooning words that could have been sung to their lovers. As Lowell Hart stated,

> music that imitates the world's music should not be used for worship
> and praise. The purpose of pop music is to entertain, not to create
> a spiritual blessing... pop music cannot create an atmosphere of

worship. This music has great appeal, but this appeal is directed toward the body, not the mind or spirit.[4]

The music of many of today's churches calls us to serve a party god. Instead of holy music, we now use music which is very much like the world's music. It should be God-centred, not self-centred.

Music in church has become a performance. A non-believer once tried to interest me in going to the church she was attending by telling me, "It's not really like a church; it's just like a show!" Is this really what God desires? Does He want church to be just like a show, where the audience sits in comfort to watch a few youth sing and preach? Are we to be mere viewers of worship, rather than intimately involved in the worship of our Creator? If this lady's church was like other churches we've visited, the congregation was left in dim lighting while the stage was lit up, with monitor speakers for the singers to hear themselves with. The main singer would be young, stylishly dressed, and holding a microphone. The congregation would listen to the music, swayed and danced to it, but probably didn't sing much.

In the churches, often there is an amplified worship team leading the singing. Because the volume is so loud, those in the congregation can hardly hear themselves over the music coming from the speakers. They can't hear their neighbours singing, and the rhythms are hard to follow. Therefore, it is becoming more and more common that the worship leaders are the only ones singing. What difference does it make if we sing, seems to be the attitude from the congregation, if the leaders are the only ones we can hear anyway, and if we can't sing the words at the right time because the rhythms are too hard? This is a very disheartening development in the life of the church. If church members are not able to participate in godly music sung to a holy God, they have lost something most precious. Over and over in the Scriptures, God calls His people to sing: Sing unto him, sing psalms unto him, talk ye of all his wondrous works. (I Chronicles 16:9) Sing praises to the LORD, which dwelleth in Zion: declare among the people his doings. (Psalm 9:11) Sing unto the LORD, O ye saints of his, and give thanks at the remembrance of his holiness. (Psalm 30:4) For God is the King of all the earth: sing ye praises with understanding. (Psalm 47:7) Sing unto the LORD; for he hath done excellent things: this is known in all the earth. (Isaiah 12:5) Sing unto the LORD a new song, and his praise from the end of the earth ... (Isaiah 42:10) Sing unto the LORD, praise ye the LORD: for he hath delivered the poor from the hand of evildoers. (Jeremiah 20:13) Speaking to yourselves in psalms and hymns and spiritual songs, singing and making melody in your heart to the Lord. (Ephesians 5:19) ... teaching and admonishing one another in psalms and hymns and spiritual songs, singing with grace in your hearts to the Lord. (Colossians 3:16) This is just a small collection of the many commands we find in Scripture to sing to the Lord. What a shame to deny this privilege in the face of overpowering performances from the stage of the local church. One of the hallmarks of the Reformation was reinstating congregational singing. May we not lose the blessing of singing to God as a body in these dark days.

A traditional church which chooses to depart from singing only hymns will typically first utilize soft rock in their services. Few Christians will immediately notice the moral issues involved in this form of music. They might speak up, but they will be silenced by the musicians and the church leaders. Some leaders will decide to evaluate each song on its own merits. As the pastors or elders listen to more and more of these songs, they become accustomed to the music's sound, and as they get used to it, they will grow to accept more strident rhythms and fleshly impact. Instead of listening to a greater amount of CCM, these leaders should have immersed themselves in the study of music and Scripture, so that they could discover the principles by which God wants them to judge the music that is used in their churches.

Only after those Christians with the most conservative musical beliefs have left the church, and the other believers have changed their tastes in church music, will the "worship" team start producing truly edgy music. And where did the conservative Christians go? They left the church into which they had invested the best of their lives to search for a safe place in which to continue raising their children. But safe churches are getting harder and harder to find. Christians who leave the church over music issues sometimes forsake the assembling of God's people altogether, or they will succumb to the lure of rock music and rationalize that it didn't matter that much after all, and rejoin the church. Another heartbreaking option that I have seen too many times is the situation where the parents continue taking the family to a church with fleshly musical standards. They try to teach their children what is right, but it does no good. Since the church with the rocky music is good enough for their parents to attend, and none of their friends at that church have any problem with the music, their children become entrapped in the very music their parents once tried to guard them against. Once they're old enough, they will likely become involved in rockier and edgier CCM, and typically, their manner of dress and their lifestyles will reflect their listening habits.

There are those who will justify the music they use in their church services because it isn't as bad as the world's music. Oh—no, it isn't. Not yet. It will be, in ten years. In a decade, the music in church will be the same as the music of the world is now, if the current trajectory of music development is followed. Christian musicians tend to present music that their congregants are already familiar with through exposure to the world's music, rather than keeping current in their musical developments. The result is that the music of the modern church tends to be around ten years behind the world's current music. Ten years from now, we still won't be too bad, comparatively speaking. The world's music will have progressed even further into carnality in those ten years, so we still won't be as carnal as they are. Tell me: what advantage is there of being just as bad as the world, but ten years behind the times?

If there is no morality in music, then why don't we sing just like the world? Part of the reason is that the congregation would be too shocked. Slowly changing church music reminds us of the frog who, being placed in lukewarm water, doesn't move as the water is slowly heated. He doesn't realize that he is being slowly boiled to death. However, if one were to drop a frog into a pan of hot water, he would immediately try to jump out. Perhaps we just feel a need to believe we're a bit better than the world is. If we play music just like they do, that would be too much—but if we play music that they used to play and that we've heard enough to become accustomed to it, we are deceived into thinking that we're not as bad as they are, because our music isn't as loud and raucous as theirs is. Our music shouldn't just be behind the times—it should be radically different than music produced by sinners who are on their way to hell. Our music should show that our citizenship is in heaven. Our melodies, rhythms, harmonies, and lyrics should reflect the beauty of heaven and God

Himself. We should not be parroting what we hear in the world—we should be seeking to perfect music that is excellent in quality and style, to the glory of God. John MacArthur states:

> Our music cannot be like the music of the world, because our God is not like their gods. Most of the world's music reflects the world's ways, the world's standards, the world's attitudes, the world's gods. To attempt to use such music to reach the world is to lower the gospel in order to spread the gospel. If the world hears that our music is not much different from theirs, it will also be inclined to believe that the Christian way of life is not much different from theirs... The music of much of the Western world is the music of seduction and suggestiveness, a musical counterpart of the immoral, lustful society that produces, sings, and enjoys it.[5]

Rick Warren wrote, "Once you have decided the style of music for your worship you have set the direction of your church in far more ways than you realize."[6]

Again, John MacArthur expounds,

> It should be noted that the many contemporary entertainers who think they are using their rock-style music to evangelize the lost are often doing nothing more than contributing to the weakening of the church. Evangelizing with contemporary music has many serious flaws. It tends to create pride in the musicians rather than humility... It makes the public proclaimers of Christianity those who are popular and talented in the world's eyes, rather than those who are godly and gifted teachers of God's truth... It creates a wide generation gap in the church, thus contributing to the disunity and lack of intimacy in the fellowship of all believers. It leads to the propagation of bad or weak theology and drags the name of the Lord down to the level of the world.[7]

Instead of seeking to win the lost by becoming like them in music, in dress, and in lifestyle, shouldn't we simply follow God in holiness? Those who are seeking will be drawn to people who obviously have something different than the rest of the world. God is different from the world: we should be, too. Those whose hearts God is drawing to Himself will notice the difference in us, and then hear from us the way to God.

Blaise Pascal put it well:

> When everything is moving at once, nothing appears to be moving, as on board ship. When everyone is moving towards depravity, no one seems to be moving. But if someone stops, he shows up the others who are rushing on, by acting as a fixed point.[8]

That is exactly why we who hold to godly musical standards are seen as an anachronism. We are holding still in our morals while all those around us change.

Martin Luther thought that music was second in importance only to doctrine. The most important thing in a church meeting is the doctrine that is preached. But the very next thing in importance, in Luther's mind, was the music. Is the music godly? Does it lead people to an encounter with the Almighty? Or does it simply appeal to our sensual nature?

Music actually seems to have an effect on doctrine. As the morality of the music decays in our churches, the doctrine follows suit. We imperceptibly lose our grip, one by one, on doctrines such as chastity before marriage, faithfulness and monogamy in marriage, tithing, and putting only that which is holy before our eyes. "I will set no wicked thing before mine eyes ..." (Psalm 101:3a) The theology of separation from the world has given way to the teaching of tolerance. Exhortations to holiness have succumbed to a fear of being thought legalistic.

Who should be providing musical leadership in the church? Should it be teenagers and young adults who do not fulfill the requirements of elders—who perhaps aren't even Christians, but play the guitar or the drums well, and so are used to "lead worship" in church? Should we be showcasing the talents of immature Christians to make them feel appreciated? Is that what Scripture tells us? Should we not be training the young believers, and teaching them to respect and learn from their elders? A godly older Christian has much to teach the young—but in this youth-worshipping society, older Christians are often ignored and ridiculed rather than respected. It's the young and beautiful who belong on the church stage, apparently. In running church like this, we train younger believers to serve themselves, to indulge in their own desires, and to be self-important. This is not training in godliness! First Timothy 3:6 describes the character of those who should be chosen for church leadership positions. God calls on us to be careful about who *not* to choose: "Not a novice, lest being lifted up with pride he fall into the condemnation of the devil." There are many temptations to pride set before the youth when they are centre stage in leading music. Timothy, the relatively youthful church leader, was encouraged to be "an example of the believers, in word, in conversation, in charity, in spirit, in faith, in purity." (I Timothy 4:12) Are we careful to only choose music leaders whose lives we would like our children to emulate? I *do* believe that only those who have ability in music should be leading congregational singing, but in addition to musical ability, we need to insure that those in charge of the music program at church and those who prominently lead music have the experience and biblical wisdom to lead the flock correctly. We need to ensure that they're not just going to tickle our ears, but that they have the edification of the saints in mind.

Even some of the older "worship leaders" in church are not known for leading a life consistent with biblical principles. And how many CCM artists have been involved in divorce, remarriage, drug use, or promiscuity? Are these really the people best suited to creating songs to glorify the God of all holiness? What must He think of us, sending Him pretty songs out of filthy hearts, or fleshly songs which do not encourage godliness? We must rethink how we do music in the church—and the music in which we immerse ourselves in our private lives.

What happens, then, when we bring this rebellious music into the church? It is no wonder that the church has fallen so far in terms of morality and attendance when we have tried for the last few decades to be just like the world.

Seduction happens slowly. If a sexual predator wants to have his way with a chaste young girl he dresses and acts respectfully, showers her with attention, and patiently woos her heart, slowly wearing down her resistance to his wiles. He convinces her of his love for her and starts to slowly stir up her passions for him. When the time comes for him to take her, she is primed and ready, and puts up little resistance. She, bit by bit, gives in to his demands. This doesn't happen overnight—it's a long, calculated set of procedures, orchestrated by someone who wants one thing, and one thing only—the conquest of someone whom no one before has been able to conquer.

The seduction of the North American church has been the same. We did not quickly jump from being a group of believers in the Lord Jesus Christ who avoided alcohol, drugs, lewdness of all kinds, immoral beliefs, and indiscreet dress, to becoming people who live wanton lives. We didn't immediately give up our belief in there being only one way to God, the concept of the Trinity, the virgin birth, and adherence to the Holy Bible as the complete, inspired Word of God. But somehow we find ourselves today with a church who dresses like the world, talks like the world, and enjoys the same entertainment as the world. Many in today's evangelical church believe that there are numerous ways to God, that premarital sex, homosexuality, and drinking are not sinful life choices, and that the Bible does not hold the answers to life. It wasn't a quick switch—it was a slow seduction.

The North American church has listened to the charming lies of the devil. The devil has convinced her that she doesn't want to be thought of as weird—that she can win people over just by being nice to them. Having softened some of the harsher doctrines, she cozies up to the world, dressing like them, talking like them, and sharing in their music and entertainment. And now that we have, for the most part, totally bought into the lie that we can belong to Christ but live like the world, we're dying. Young people are leaving the church by the thousands, and we just try to be more and more like the world in order to win them back. I don't believe they'll be returning. We've avoided godliness and renamed it legalism. We've tried to avoid offending people by neglecting the preaching of the gospel—so much that we've forgotten to preach to our own children the truth of God: that we are all sinners (Romans 3:3) and Christ offers forgiveness only through His death on the cross for us (Romans 6:23). We've imitated the world in our dress, our language, our musical styles, and our marketing strategies. If the church is just like the world—*who needs it?*

I believe that a big part of the seduction of the North American church has happened under the influence of the devil's musical talents. He didn't come charging into the twentieth century church with punk and rap and screamo. No, he exposed Christians to entertainment that really wasn't that bad, and music featuring crooners like Frankie Avalon and Tony Bennett. After one generation of the church had become accustomed to the music of the world, the next generation started asking for new types of music to be sung in the churches. There was nothing wrong with much of the Scripture song movement, or with many of the songs and choruses that sprang up in the 70's and 80's. The older folks felt that there was something amiss with some of the new music, but most couldn't quite put their finger on it, because, after all, it must be good to sing Bible verses—isn't it? The younger generation started to go to concerts featuring Christian music they weren't hearing in their churches, and by the time *their* children had reached adolescence, they found ready hearers as they demanded to replace the hymns with the current CCM. By the early years of the twenty-first century, hymns had practically disappeared from the modern church in North America. And so, while there hasn't been a sudden takeover, there has been a steady shift in the direction of edgier forms of music, amounting to the infiltration and seduction of the church by a new music ideology.

Musicians through the centuries have always produced new music, changing forms and modalities, and stretching known musical boundaries. Few of them ever caused riots or experienced concertgoers calling their music immoral. There are innumerable ways in which to arrange and create new music which do not require us to descend into ungodliness.

> Bach the scholar and prototype of a composition professor conceived his music for the benefit of those who did not 'confuse important ideas with childish notions' and 'whose musical hearing is not spoiled by ... newfangled taste.'[9]

He who quite possibly produced more new music than any other composer in history was able to discern between music with important ideas and that which flaunted newfangled taste. The need to practice discernment when evaluating new music did not end with Bach. We must not accept a song or a musical style just because it's new and in vogue. Choosing worldly things that make us seem more fashionable or modern, that make us fit in with our peers better, is not something God respects. We also must not reject music simply because it is new; we must evaluate all music—indeed, all of life—by biblical principles.

In evaluating music biblically, we must avoid relying solely on our emotions. How many times have I heard statements like, "This music speaks to my heart," or "I was touched by that music," or "I live for that music!" We cannot choose to accept or reject music based on our emotional response.

It does no good to say that the music we listen to isn't as bad as that which others listen to. If rock music is a road that leads to ungodliness, what does it matter whether you go one hundred miles down that road or three thousand? Every believing Christian ought to have as his primary goal serving God and becoming more like Him. If listening to rock music leads one to ungodliness, it ought to be avoided altogether. Because the human heart is deceitful, we are often not as well qualified to determine our spiritual growth as others are. In evaluating our listening habits, we must not rationalize that we only listen to the soft stuff and avoid the really hard stuff. God demands that we avoid evil influences entirely!

An alcoholic doesn't tend to get totally inebriated the first time he experiences alcohol. He might have some sips of wine as a child, drink a few beers when he becomes a teenager, buy his own alcohol once he nears legal age, and in time he is consuming hard liquor regularly. In the same way, the average conservative churchgoer who decides to put up with a little soft rock will, before too long, branch out into more strident, rhythmically dominated music. It doesn't take long to go from the smooth, mellow sounds of Mercy Me to the much more driven sounds of 33 Miles.

When we first married in 1990, my husband and I went to a small church with very traditional forms of music. The music in the first service consisted of hymns sung a capella, and the music in the second service was accompanied by a piano and perhaps an organ. My husband became a deacon and the Sunday school superintendent; I taught Sunday school. We had our first two children while attending that church, then left for four years to attend Bible school. We returned to that church with a Bible college education and three more children. I led the choir, and we were both involved in the Sunday school. A few years after our return, we heard that the youth had started up a music group. Naively, we assumed that they would be singing a capella, or performing godly songs with accompaniment for the congregation. The elders made several changes in church function and doctrine around that time—serious changes which disturbed us. But we weren't expecting what came next. We were shocked when the youth group stood up to perform. There were several of them—kids we had known since infancy or childhood. Some of them had worked in our ministry, and others we didn't know quite as well. They went up front with their keyboard and electric guitar. Several of them stood up front—in a small church, it seemed unnatural and overwhelming to have that many people leading a song. Then the music started—drum accompaniments, syncopated, breathy singing—they might as well have been singing in a bar.

We left that service soon after they started, and in the next week or two, my husband wrote a letter to the elders, describing our dismay that they had made so many important changes in so little time, with no input from the congregation, to the best of our knowledge. The board of elders demanded a meeting. It was more like an inquisition, really. They defended the changes they had made in doctrine, practice, and music and removed from us any ability to minister at church. I was forbidden to teach Sunday school. We, as parents, were forbidden to check on our children when Sunday school was in session. My husband was not allowed to speak publicly at any church event. Our children were not allowed to play the piano for meetings or lead the singing, though others of their age and ability were encouraged to.

We continued attending this church, putting up with more sensuality in the music than we should have, and quietly walking out of services when it just got to be too much to put up with. The "instrumentalists" and singers introduced sensual beats as they led the congregation in songs which were sometimes devoid of theological meaning. I remember looking around when a new song was introduced and seeing that only the youth, who had heard this song in the context of radio, music download, or youth group many times before, were singing along. No one else could follow the syncopated rhythms.

We endured this shunning for ten painful years before the blatant dishonesty of an elder clinched the decision to find another church. After some searching, we found a church with great preaching, sweet fellowship, and beautiful music. Finding ourselves at home there, we became members. A year or so later, another couple joined the church. He had a theology degree; she had a master's degree in music. Together they took over the music of the church. The hymn books were ditched in favour of the overhead projector. Now, there's nothing wrong with overheads. When used to facilitate singing, they encourage people to keep their heads up, which allows for better projection of the voice. However, it's hard to display hymns with their music on a projector. Gradually the hymns were replaced by CCM songs. The rhythms went from being regular and singable to being syncopated and rocky. A sound system was added to this small church. When people complained about the volume hurting their ears, their pleas to have the sound turned down were ignored or ridiculed. Congregants stopped singing. What did it matter? The volume from the performers up front was so loud that you couldn't hear yourself or your neighbour sing anyway. Soon there was only one hymn per service, along with several modern songs. Some of these newer songs were great—some of them were fleshly. There were more and more songs in which we could not participate. The preaching suffered. The fellowship waned. Another event occurred, unrelated to issues of morality in the church, that led us out and into another church.

Although I've mentioned only three churches in this brief story, we ended up visiting dozens of churches. In our search for a church home, we came close to losing hope that we would ever find a church that still employed any discernment in the music they used. Thank God there are still a few left.

If Martin Luther was right, and congregational singing is an indispensable part of church function, then what have we done by making music the realm of a few talented individuals whose volume is increased to the point of pain, and of discouraging anyone else from singing? We have basically reproduced part of the problem with music that Luther was objecting to. Before the Reformation in Europe, music in church was relegated to the choir. No one in the congregation sang or was expected to. Music was presented simply as a performance by trained individuals. Martin Luther, though, believed that singing was a gift of God that should be shared with all Christians. His emphasis on chorales which the entire congregation would sing was revolutionary at the time. He would be aghast to see how far we have fallen from the truths embraced by the Reformation.

Why does music cause conflict? There may be disagreements in a church about the colour of the carpet or the choice of a pastor, but few things in recent decades have caused as much conflict and division as has the choice of musical style in a church. Because music impacts our innermost being, those who reject the music we like can seem to be rejecting us. In addition, it is hard for most people to articulate the elements of music which they find uncomfortable, and which can lead to ungodly thoughts and lifestyles. Since they can't explain these musical elements, even to themselves, people begin to believe that they are wrong, and give up the convictions they once held in the area of music. In the meantime, disregarding all logic and the wisdom of the aged, those who desire CCM in church force their way with arguments and name-calling that polite conservative members are too shocked to confront.

Let's face it: those of us with conservative musical convictions are in the minority. Not only that, but most of us don't have the debate skills to be able to soundly convince the naysayers that there is value in godly music, and danger in listening to that which is lascivious. Most people who know in their hearts that there's a problem with much modern music don't have the training they feel they need in order to argue their case. And so they remain silent. The opposition to this issue is strong. Who wants to be the lone dissenting voice in an argument that seems lost already? Which frumpy middle-aged housewife wants to seem an old-fashioned stodge when presenting the facts to glamourous and popular youth who rule the stage? It's a battle that most of us, frankly, have given up.

I recently attended an event connected with our ministry, which I had helped to organize and was contributing to with my personal finances. I had, unfortunately, not shown enough caution in the supervision of the musicians chosen. During a rehearsal, I noticed one of the musicians playing a song which was highly syncopated. The moment he began playing, the other participants in the event began dancing in a sensual manner. Most of these were upstanding young Christian adults—and yet, just a few notes into very syncopated music, their base natures were appealed to so strongly that they immediately began responding bodily. My husband and I privately spoke to this young musician later. We kindly expressed our desire for him to adjust his music to a more traditional feel—more playing on the beat rather than off the beat. Unfortunately, the music of our culture is almost completely given over to this kind of rhythmic arrangement—so much so that this young man, though he was musically gifted and tried really hard to understand, had great difficulty in producing anything but the sound in which he'd been immersing himself for years. His attitude was stellar, wanting to cooperate and honour our request—and yet, despite his best efforts, he was able to make very few improvements to the music by the time he performed it for the attendees of the event.

During a wedding I attended a couple of years ago, I witnessed the same thing. The music matched the attitude of the beautiful, reverent service—until the bride and groom walked back down the aisle together. The music chosen for that part of the service was driving and sensual. Immediately—within a second or so of the beginning of the music, the congregation was swaying their hips and moving in other sensual ways. This movement marked a huge change from their behaviour during the rest of the service—and it was obviously driven by the music.

The attitude of the first musician, who tried to change his music when we requested him to do so, was remarkable. We identify with our chosen music so forcefully—so personally—that if someone is to criticize anything about the music we like, we react as if we have received a personal attack. In past, when I have mentioned the effects of rock music to individuals, they have responded with anything from curiosity to polite disagreement to violent defamation. There are some individuals who have received the information thoughtfully— and I dearly value those responses. But because I know the reaction I am likely to get, I rarely bring the subject up, and expect attacks when I do. Therefore, the writing of this book is done with prayerful conviction.

I believe that God intends for good music to be sung by all the Christians at church, internalized by all, and used in communal worship. We mustn't go to church to see a show or to be entertained. We must go to have fellowship, to be taught God's truth, and to sing together—to reinforce biblical teaching with the words of the music, to experience godly melodies that fasten those truths in our heads, and to involve our souls in the worship of the One True God.

As this book is about to go to print, we are six months into Covid-19. Most churches were closed for months, and many jurisdictions forbade congregational singing after the churches were allowed to open. How we have missed it! Our souls felt lean after months of little face-to-face fellowship, and no singing together as groups of believers. What a relief it was, what a joy, to be able to join in song once again!

Music is an inherent part of our spiritual beings. We must praise God in song to be spiritually whole. Let us ensure that the songs with which we praise God are a balm to His Spirit and a pure blessing to ours.

CHAPTER 13

What to do about Disagreements

When Paul wrote the book of Romans, he discussed the disagreements between Christians as to whether to eat meat sacrificed to idols or not. Paul told them that no matter what they believed about the issue, they were to remember that their brothers and sisters in Christ were of more value than their own rights to eat as they chose. He told them to avoid offending other Christians. Paul said that he would eat no meat while the world stood, rather than offend another Christian.

How many of us are willing to obey the Scripture in this matter? We are extremely careful not to offend those with more liberal convictions than we have. We've changed our language in order to not affront those who identify with alternative lifestyle choices. We have watered down doctrines on co-habitation, immodest dress, and alcohol consumption so that we don't displease those who feel that they can involve themselves in those activities without guilt. But what do we do when someone we know has a belief that is more conservative than ours? Whether it's in the matter of modest dress, head-covering, distinctions between the roles of men and women in the church, divorce and remarriage, or music, the more conservative person is challenged to prove his position in the Scriptures, while the more liberal one is not. The conservative Christian is often marginalized and ostracized, passed over and ignored because of his views. Usually other Christians don't even bother asking about why these more conservative Christians believe as they do.

Rather than labelling our brothers and sisters in Christ legalists because they have more traditional beliefs, why don't we engage them in kind, interested discussion as to why they believe as they do? Perhaps those who have adopted the liberal views that were largely unheard of in Christians fifty to a hundred years ago should do some serious rethinking of their own views. At least let's stop calling other believers legalists. A true legalist is one who believes that his good behaviour of any kind is going to get him to heaven. A legalist in terms of dress might be one who believes that any woman who wears a skirt with a hemline above the knees is not going to heaven. A legalist when it comes to music might believe that no one who listens to contemporary Christian music will be found in heaven, and that his own discernment in music is going to permit him access to heaven. But really—that's not what's going on here. Those who believe that music has moral value have a point of view different than the majority of the Western church. They know that. They have probably already suffered ridicule, a loss of friends, and a loss of ministry opportunities because of their views. Let's not assume that they are legalistic, nor that they are ignorant of the permissive musical views of most of North American Christianity. Let's not assume that they know nothing about modern Christian music. Instead, let us engage them, learn from them, pray about the information we receive from them, study all Scripture pertaining to the topic, and then make a decision that is in line with God's will.

Those who have more liberal views than we have are not necessarily godless individuals who are intending to subvert the world! Some have never honestly given a thought to having musical discernment.

Years ago I had a friend named Carol. Though Carol and her husband had issues, I never heard Carol speak a negative word about him—or about anyone else. She encouraged me to honour my parents and she faithfully raised her two girls. She was faithful at church and heroically persevered through many difficulties. Carol also smoked rather heavily. I could have judged Carol for smoking and disregarded all the other evidence that pointed to her spiritual maturity. If I had done that, I would have been missing a treasure. Carol was a brand plucked from the fire. After spending her childhood in the foster system, she became a Christian and sought to walk with God. Even though she smoked, I could tell that she was a better Christian than I was in many ways. Carol died of bowel cancer, leaving behind two teenaged girls and a bereaved husband. She taught me the lesson that we are not to judge our brothers and sisters in Christ harshly.

When we have made a decision that is not the same as another Christian's decision about what kind of music is appropriate, let us continue to treat them with respect. Let us be willing, as one young man I know is, to change our playlists rather than offend our brothers and sisters in Christ. Let us be willing to give up whatever earthly pleasure we need to, in order to encourage unity in the body. As soldiers of Christ, we need to willingly relinquish any fleshly entertainment that might cause our brothers to sin.

I have, in past, had friends who believed that they must always keep their hair long, wear dresses, and cover their heads. When in their company, I have worn dresses and covered my head. I have not done that to deceive them into believing that I believed just as they did. I have done so out of respect for their convictions, even though I did not believe the same way. This is simply caring consideration.

And yet, in many churches in Canada today, the young have been encouraged to play their music in the church without regard to the sensibilities of the older believers. We of a previous generation have been told that as older believers, we should show love and tolerance, and must not only permit, but even enjoy and encourage the musical offerings of the young—and that we are not to discuss morality when it comes to music. But let's re-examine that.

We must stand for the truth. Whether it is the plain truth of the gospel, the truth that is being suppressed in an argument between individuals or nations, the truth of God being smothered by propaganda, or simply the truth that bad music produces bad results and good music edifies—we must be willing to stand firm under the onslaught of fiery indignation handed to us by people who really enjoy what they are doing and would rather not hear that they are damaging themselves spiritually. We must speak truth when God gives us the opportunity to do so. The battle, in the end, is God's and not ours, and He is the only One with the power to overcome the spirit of the age.

Francis Schaeffer wrote in *How Should We Then Live*,

There is a flow to history and culture. This flow is rooted and has its wellspring in the thoughts of people. People are unique in the inner life of the mind—what they are in their thought world determines how they act. This is true of their value systems and it is true of their creativity. It is true of their corporate actions, such as political decisions, and it is true of their personal lives. The results of their thought world flow from their fingers or from their tongues into the external world. This is true of Michelangelo's chisel, and it is true of a dictator's sword.[1]

Following Shaeffer's train of thought, the way a person thinks influences what he does. If a person is full of dark, hopeless thoughts, that will show in any work of art he produces, whether a painting or a song. That painting or that song will influence the thoughts of those who see or hear it. As more and more people become influenced by the dark and hopeless thoughts expressed by an artist, these types of thoughts become part of the culture, and are expressed in more and varied ways.

The most common subjects of secular songs are love and sex. Opinions about these subjects are expressed through music and influence those who hear that music. Thoughts of this nature become normalized when great portions of society are accustomed to hearing them in their music and in other forms of artistic expression. As these sensual thoughts become mainstream, society is changed from one of nuclear families living as God intended to one of splintered families and lascivious lifestyles being glorified in the movies and, to some extent, in our churches.

What should our response as thinking, committed Christians be? Should we choose the path of least resistance, the path that appeals most to our flesh, and which will help us to avoid mistreatment by those who defend their own choices? Or should we seek the higher ground, attempting to fulfill the biblical imperative to "Be holy, for I am holy"? (I Peter 1:16) In the seventeenth century, Pastor Jeremiah Burroughs wrote, "It is a very evil choice for any soul under heaven to choose the least sin rather than the greatest affliction."[2] Can we, in our North American comfort, even begin to comprehend what that means? When is sin sin? If we know something is a sin, is it okay to indulge in it if it means we can avoid displeasing someone else by so doing? Are there some sins which really aren't that bad, and only a few which we should avoid at all costs? When we think of the cost paid by our Saviour to cleanse us from our sin, how can we then rationalize that any sin would be acceptable in His sight? When we consider the fact that He is Lord of our lives, we must willingly give Him all of us, and all of our interests and desires. We must hold nothing back. If the evidence presented in these pages has clearly presented the fact that music has power, and that it is a sin to willfully involve ourselves in something that influences us to ungodly sensuality, then we are denying the truth that Christ has revealed to us if we choose to indulge in our own selfish desires.

If we choose to follow the evidence and develop some convictions about what is and is not good music, we're going to disagree with many of our brothers and sisters in Christ. We can keep our opinions to ourselves, and sometimes this is wise. We don't need to be criticizing everyone else and arguing about musical styles with our friends. But does that mean we should just go along with what everyone else is listening to?

We are to be people of truth. Jesus Christ identified Himself as truth in John 14: "I am the way, the truth and the life." All through the Scripture, it is assumed that if we are followers of God, we will be followers of the truth. A few of the many Scriptures that discuss this thought are 2 John 2–4, Psalm 115:1, and 3 John 3, 8–12. Another powerful verse is 3 John 4: "I have no greater joy than to hear that my children walk in truth." We cannot deceive ourselves into denying the effect that music has on our souls, and especially, we must realize the spiritual influence music has when we are exposed to it regularly in a trusted environment like church.

If one finds oneself in a church where rock music is played as worship, one could try talking to the leader of the music program. There are many good books on the subject of the moral influence of music—I've listed several in the bibliography. Perhaps asking your music leader to read one of those books would be helpful. In my experience, though, it's very possible that the music leader will not be interested in considering a point of view other than his own. What do you do then? Staying in that church will harden you to the deceitfulness of sin. You will become familiar with other believers who accept fleshly music as useful in worship. If you have children, you will train them up in a way they should not go. If the music leader will not listen to your concerns, it may be time to find another church.

Through the changing music and doctrinal standards of the churches we have attended, we never left a church solely because of the music. However, our experience is that where there is sensual music used as worship music, there will also be poor doctrine and dishonesty.

Music's effects are powerful, and I regret from the bottom of my soul the impact on my children of spending ten years at a church whose music degraded into lasciviousness during their teenage years. There may come a time when you are convicted to leave a church because the music is sensual rather than spiritual. Let God guide you in that case and be honest and kind to those with whom you disagree.

Do your friends insist on playing offensive music around you? Try to have calm discussions with them about why some music is actually bad for you. People tend to be very emotional when the subject of music comes up, and many will turn on their friends for disagreeing with them on this subject. Don't shy away from the discussion. Expect opposition and pray before-hand that God will help you to stay calm and loving. II Timothy 2:19 to 3:8 has a lot to say about the subject of disagreements, whether about music or anything else.

> Let every one that nameth the name of Christ depart from iniquity. But in a great house there are not only vessels of gold and of silver, but also of wood and of earth; and some to honour, and some to dishonour. If a man therefore purge himself from these, he shall be a vessel unto honour, sanctified, and meet for the master's use, and prepared unto every good work. Flee also youthful lusts: but follow righteousness, faith, charity, peace, with them that call on the Lord out of a pure heart. But foolish and unlearned questions avoid, knowing that they do gender strifes. And the servant of the Lord must not strive; but be gentle unto all men, apt to teach, patient, In meekness instructing those that oppose themselves; if God peradventure will give them repentance to the acknowledging of the truth; And that they may recover themselves out of the snare of the devil, who are taken captive by him at his will. This know also, that in the last days perilous times shall come. For men shall be

lovers of their own selves, covetous, boasters, proud, blasphemers, disobedient to parents, unthankful, unholy, without natural affection, trucebreakers, false accusers, incontinent, fierce, despisers of those that are good, traitors, heady, highminded, lovers of pleasures more than lovers of God; having a form of godliness, but denying the power thereof: from such turn away.

This passage tells us that we are to leave sin behind. We need to do so, even if it involves throwing out music that has a sinful influence on us. It's possible that someone will strongly refuse your offer to calmly discuss music, and will forcefully present his ideas and his music. At some point you may need to part company with such a person. The Bible actually has quite a bit to say about separating ourselves from people who are consistently involved in certain sins without repentance. We are told in this passage to flee youthful lusts and cling to that which is good, WITH others who are following the Lord out of a pure heart! Find yourself some good friends who either have conservative musical convictions, or at least will not push their views and their music on you. We are told to avoid arguments, but be gentle, patient, able to teach those whose beliefs are harming them. Pray that God will grant them understanding and repentance! There follows a list of descriptions which succinctly describe people in the current generation. They are despisers of those who are good. If you make a choice to listen to only God-honouring music, there will be those who will despise you. Jesus also lived through this sort of situation: because He was totally good, there were those who despised Him. He goes with you through every difficult event in your life. Music has such a powerful hold on people that they resist any truth that might threaten their listening habits. Expect that—don't be surprised by it—and keep loving the people anyway.

A good friend of mine has a husband who is on the worship team of their church. He is a talented guitar player who plays many forms of music. Their entire family is very musical, and has performed at events associated with our ministry. And yet, their musical convictions are entirely different than ours. We have agreed to disagree on this issue. She doesn't play music when I'm around, and we don't argue about the topic. When minor issues do come up, the topic is changed quickly. We know where each other stands, and we just choose to enjoy our friendship without having to agree about music. This is a great option for some people. If you can be friends without offending one another, do so. However, if a friend insists on playing ungodly music whenever you're around even though he knows you believe it to be spiritually harmful, and argues with you repeatedly about whether there's any morality in music at all, it's time to re-evaluate that relationship.

CHAPTER 14
How to Be Freed from a Music Addiction

It's difficult to admit that you're addicted. Whether it's tobacco, alcohol, drugs, computer gaming, or rock music, we think we can quit any time we want. In actual fact, doing it is much harder than we might think.

Listening to rock music can be an addictive behaviour. There are people who listen to rock music so much that to listen to any other kind of music results in headaches. These people have to fill every free moment with their music. This is an unhealthy addiction.

In Deuteronomy 6:5, God commands the children of Israel, "Thou shalt love the Lord thy God with all thy heart, and with all thy soul, and with all thy strength, and with all thy mind …" In case we thought this command was only for the Israelites, God repeats it in the New Testament in Luke 10:27. Did you notice the four times the word "all" is used in this verse? If we are to love the Lord our God with ALL our heart, soul, strength, and mind—every bit of it—we need to make sure we identify God's will for us in every area of our lives, and then do it. We can't ignore the possibility that CCM has an evil influence over us. We can't just assume that it doesn't, and carry on as if all is well. If we are truly living this verse as God intended, we will carefully and honestly examine the issue, and then live in obedience to Him.

As was mentioned earlier in this book, I know a young man who said of CCM, "I LIVE for that music!" This young man was a music leader in his church. There is actually no music on earth worth the total investment of our lives. We ought to be living for the Lord, and ready to do or refrain from doing anything He tells us to.

There's a difference I've noticed between lovers of classical music and lovers of rock music. The lovers of more traditional styles of music also enjoy silence. They are pleased by the singing of the birds, or the rustling of the wind in the trees. Those who show an addiction to rock music, however, are rarely without their music. Their ear buds are worn while walking, taking the bus, or sitting around. If they are able to, they spend huge amounts of money on concerts. They seem to have a need to be listening to their music for most of the day. Now, I love good music. It can cheer my heart to sing "Lead On, O King Eternal," or to listen to Bach's *Little Fugue*. But I have no need to be surrounded by music at all times. Whenever we feel like we need something all the time, we should wonder about its power over us.

Whether or not you think you're addicted to rock music in any of its forms, it will be helpful for you to experience some time without it. If you have a friend with reliably conservative musical standards, you could ask him or her to help you go through your music collection. Use the methods given in chapter 15, "How to Discern Good Music," to remove from your collection any music that doesn't seem totally pure and godly. You might not be ready to actually throw all the remaining music out just yet. I think it's best to throw it out before you second guess yourself! But if you can't quite bring yourself to do that, put the music away where you won't have access to it for at least a month. Save the good music. There might be whole CDs or entire MP3's that you can keep. You might want to record only a few worthy songs from an album which also contains questionable music.

For at least one month, listen only to good music. Listen to the good parts of your collections. Download some free classical music online. Check the appendix at the end of this book for suggested resources. Borrow good music from the library or conservative friends. Listen to music as much as you previously did, but make it good music instead of listening to sensual sounds. Don't forget to enjoy some silence, too—as much as you like. Avoid going to places where you know there will be unwholesome music. This means that, for a month, you'll stay away from the mall, restaurants, the houses of some friends and acquaintances, etc. If you have to be near rocky music, take your earbuds along to fill your soul with good music instead. When watching movies or TV shows, use the mute button whenever there is unwholesome music in the sound track. Better yet, curtail your viewing habits for a month. Keep your mind and heart totally free of rock music for at least four weeks.

If the addiction is strong, you may experience headaches while you withdraw from the rock music. Your brain will be having a hard time getting along without its unhealthy musical fix. Drink extra water and rest when you need to. You'll get over the headaches if you can stick with the good music.

At first the conservative music might make you feel anxious. Think of a heroin addict trying to live without his fix. He's nervous, sweaty and agitated. Your tension will pass. Keep the classical music fairly quiet if you find it bothersome. Try different kinds of good music until you find something you like, even a little.

If your addiction is severe and you've experienced headaches, keep on the rock music "fast" for a month after your last headache.

During your month of good music, and after your agitation subsides, keep track of your emotions and interactions with others. You might not notice any change. Ask those close to you—a spouse, a parent, a friend, if they've noticed any recent changes in you at the end of your month without rock.

After at least a month without rock music, you might choose to listen to your old music again. I think that you will find that it sounds harsher and less lovely than it did before your month off. Your taste for it may have reduced in intensity. However, if you make a habit of listening to all the old music again, your addiction will come back full force. If what I have written in this book makes sense, and you believe that there is music that is bad for you, then just throw out your CDs. Delete your MP3s. Start afresh. Ask for specific music for your birthday and Christmas—ask for music that will uplift your soul and edify your spirit.

We do live in this world, and worldly music pervades civilization almost entirely. When you cannot avoid it, steel yourself against the effect it tries to have on your soul, and pray for God's protection. I believe that fleshly music is one of the "works of darkness" that Romans 13:12 tells us to cast off. We are told in Ephesians 5 to walk as children of light, and exhibit the righteous fruit of the Spirit. Verse ten tells us to prove what is acceptable to the Lord. That means to discern, to judge, to investigate honestly until you find out what is truly acceptable to the Lord. We are not to have any fellowship with the unfruitful works of darkness—avoid those places where you'll be involved in listening to sensual music. Considering our discussion of addiction, it's interesting that this passage which compares light to darkness then admonishes us to not be drunk with wine, which can also have addicting power. The very next verse tells us to speak to ourselves in psalms and hymns and spiritual songs, singing and making melody in our hearts to the Lord. Replace any fleshly music in your life with good quality music. Psalms set to music and hymns are usually pretty safe when considering music that is good for you. Spiritual songs must be spiritual—both in music and in lyrics. Paul writes in II Corinthians 6:14, "What communion hath light with darkness?" We mustn't mix spiritual words with ungodly rhythms.

And finally, in Ephesians 5:20, we are told to be thankful. Following the righteousness of God requires that we be thankful for the opportunity to do so—not pining after the music we used to listen to. That would only lead to relapse. Instead, choose to enjoy godly music, and thank God for the ability to hear and enjoy it. Thank Him for the skills of the musicians who wrote the good music you're listening to, and thank Him that He created music for us to enjoy. Remember that God is able to make all things new, and He will bless your efforts to clean up your music if you let Him.

CHAPTER 15
How to Discern Good Music

Discernment. It's a big word, and it's a huge challenge to try to live our lives in this world, in this society, with the ability to discern between good and evil. Whether it's language, entertainment, clothes, or music, the Holy Spirit and the Word of God are our Guides to living this life in a way that pleases God. We are told in Hebrews 5:14 that strong meat belongeth to them that are of full age, even those who by reason of use have their senses exercised to discern both good and evil. Notice that our senses must be used to discern whether objects and activities are good or evil. As we consider each item in our wardrobe or our play list, let us fall under the Holy Spirit's guidance as we use our senses to determine what to keep and what to throw out.

If you have been convinced that there are forms of music that are good for you and forms of music that are bad for you, you're going to have to develop discernment so that you can tell what kind of music you should be listening to. Much of that information you will have picked up from the earlier parts of this book.

There are two basic forms of music I'm going to discuss that you shouldn't be listening to because of their negative effects on your morals. You can start your basic classification of music by dividing the song in question into one of three groups: rock, jazz, or square.

Just as a carpenter has to have a reliable square, and an engineer needs to follow certain formulas and have a solid frame of reference before he starts building a bridge, music needs to be based on a solid, square beat pattern in order to be safe to use as a building block for our souls. For our characters are built by the habits that we form and the sensory experiences we undergo. The pattern of **1**–2–**3**–4 that was mentioned earlier in this book is the time-tested, reliable pattern for 4/4 time that works and does not elicit ungodly sensual responses from its listeners. In 3/4 time, you would be listening for a strong first beat and two weak beats, typically expressed in a **1**–2–3 pattern. Often a performer will stress every second beat **1** in a song in 3/4 time. This has the same effect as rock music—it is a form of rock music. Another way of counting such an arrangement of music in 3/4 time would be **1**–2–3 **2**–2–3 **3**–2–3 **4**–2–3. This is just a more complicated version of the rock pattern 1–**2**–3–**4**. Avoid musical pieces which utilize this stress on alternate first beats of music in 3/4 time. There are various sub-genres of rock music, such as hip-hop, acid, soft rock, and screamo. Each of these has qualities which differentiate it from other forms of rock, but they will all have a beat pattern which stresses the second and fourth beats in a bar of music.

But how do you tell where the beats lie in music that you're listening to? It's really easy with baroque or classical music, because your toes will want to tap on the beat. The first beat will be a little stronger. Try listening to some march music. In Sousa's marching band music, the first and third beats are often accentuated with a bass drum. They're the naturally stressed beats in those forms of music. As a matter of fact, I just turned on a Sousa march, and one daughter started swinging her head to the music and another got up and started marching!

But in rock music? It seems like everything's stressed *but* the first beat. Here's a tip, though. Listen to the keyboard. Typically the chord will change on the first beat. Sometimes there will be a repeating chord progression that will start again on each first beat. Whether the instrumental music is produced by the keyboard or the guitar, the biggest changes will happen on beat one. Although it is not the point of this book to encourage you to listen to sensual music, it would be helpful for you to have some examples of what

I'm trying to explain, as it is difficult to adequately describe musical concepts with words alone.

Find the song *Hold Me Now* by Hillsong United on YouTube. Near the end of that song, the words "need you now" and "soul cries out" are sung on beats 1, 2 and 3. Listen to the electric guitar. It repeats a lot of notes, and usually only changes notes in this section on beat one.

Now find the YouTube video of Kristin Getty singing *The Lord is My Salvation*. Choose the one with the scene of the sea beating against the shore, with guitar chords on the bottom right. The song starts with four one-beat chords on a keyboard followed by another chord on a long note. These two bars repeat two times, then Kristin starts singing. Notice that the words "the solid rock" are solidly placed on beats one, two, and three. Then the percussion is added with a rock beat. If you've been counting 1–2–3–4 up to this point, you can now hear that the snare drum is sounded on beats 2 and 4, making this a rock song. Kristin often sings on beat one, and there are often chord changes on beat one.

Now find *Grace* by CityAlight. The song starts with eight long notes—each note is four beats long. The first line is, with emphasis on each beat: "Your **grace** that **leads** this **sinner home**." It's easy to see where the beats lie in this song, and it has no emphasis on off-beats, which would, if they were there, create more of a sensual effect.

Go back and listen to all three of these songs again and notice the difference each makes to your soul and senses. If you don't notice a difference, maybe you should go read Chapter 14 again. <insert smiley face>

Jazz music is meant to break down inhibitions—those aversions God has built into us which help us to avoid things that we know will be pleasurable immediately but bring heartbreak in the long run. These inhibitions are actually helpful for godly living, so breaking them down is not an aid to righteousness. It is no coincidence that jazz musicians have a reputation for an involvement in easy sex and imbibing alcohol and drugs. Jazz is identified by the fact that beats are not evenly divided, but rather, each set of two notes is given different lengths. The first note will be longer and the second shorter. So, instead of a set of eighth notes sounding dah dah dah dah dah dah dah dah, in jazz music it will be more like daaah da daaah da daaah da daaah da.

Jazz music utilizes the saxophone more often than rock or classical music. Some sub-genres of jazz are big band, boogie-woogie, and the blues.

Both rock and jazz utilize singing techniques meant to sound sensual, thereby eliciting sensuality in the hearers. Sliding is a term used to describe what a vocalist does when she sings from one note to another, across many notes of the scale, as a constant slide; rather than singing one note at a time in an ascending scale. Think of the way a siren goes from a note further down the scale to one higher up. You're driving in traffic and hear that low start to the siren. It catches your attention and you listen as it slides it way upward through several notes of the scale, then slides back down again, repeating itself endlessly as the emergency vehicle tries to get to its destination. Think of how a trombone can go from one note to another by moving the slide without tonguing—from low to high in a steady upwards direction. Both of these examples demonstrate sliding. Another technique used to encourage lasciviousness is a breathy voice. When I was going to university, my choral professor told us that young, untrained voices tend to be breathy. He told us it's a normal thing, and it shows lack of musical training, because too much air is getting past the vocal cords without being properly utilized. Nowadays, though, breathiness is used on purpose to sound sensual.

They say sex sells. The music industry has taken this to heart. Almost every-thing about popular music, "Christian" or not, screams sex. From the clothes worn by the musicians, to the lowered light levels, to the vocal techniques—all are reminiscent of people engaging in intimate acts. Is this attitude towards free sex what we really want to encourage in our Christian youth? Or anyone else, for that matter? Sex is a blessing given by God to married couples. It's not to be cheapened, sold on stage, or encouraged to be used by just anybody whenever they feel like it. It's a precious gift and should be treated as such. When we awaken those desires in people who are unmarried, we are defrauding them—cheating them of the perfect scenario for this blessing by making it common and easy. The strong draw of the sensual effects of this music overrides our senses and our thoughts, encouraging us to fixate on this one facet of our existence. It's not that sex and sexuality are wrong! It's that they are cheapened and perverted by strutting them on stage for all to see—or promoting sexuality over the radio, TV, CDs, MP3s, and church stages in the form of music.

And sex isn't the only thing promoted by rock and jazz music. Drinking, drugs, violence, and rebellion are all encouraged by the underlying message communicated by the music that most of us in North America are listening to. Is it our place to contribute to the fall of our society by packaging up this sensual rebellion in Christian words and calling it CCM? God forbid.

The third form of music, the sounds we should be filling our heads and hearts with, is square. By "square," I mean that the notes all have their proper value. The beats fall on the proper places. In 4/4 time the beats will be sounded as **1**–2–**3**–4, or in 3/4 time they will be **1**–2–3. There will be little to no breathiness or other sensual effects in singing, and the words will be at least inoffensive, and at best truly edifying. There will be harmony, beautiful melodies, and measured rhythms all meant to encourage our souls in emotion, in rational thought, in godliness. Please see the appendix for a list of music you can use to feed your spirit with beauty and order—to exercise your senses by filling them with good music.

May God bless us as we seek to serve Him with ALL our hearts, ALL our souls, ALL our minds, and ALL our strength. And may we love our neighbours as ourselves as we share with them beautiful examples of music that they may never have heard before.

Edifying, Enjoyable Music

Music is such an integral element in human beings that we will seek it out or create it ourselves. If you have decided that some of your music must go, please don't just leave a void; replace the music you're getting rid of with rich music that uplifts your soul!

Anything new is awkward. Think of the first time you rode a bike, made a latte, or drove a car. Your determination to learn made you continue the activity, but it might not have been very pleasurable until you developed the skills you needed. When I started feeding my babies solid food, they didn't necessarily like it at first. I knew they needed to eat regular food, so I continued introducing good foods to them. As they've grown, they've all developed different tastes in food: some like mushrooms while others can't stand them. One would eat nothing but fruit if I would let her. But we all agree that certain foods are junk foods, low in nutrition and high in calories, and should be eaten, if at all, in moderation. We also know that some things that look like foods are in fact poison (some mushrooms, some berries, some leaves). Eating these would cause harm.

As children need to learn to appreciate healthy eating, adults need to develop a taste for good music. If you've been listening to nothing but modern forms of popular music all your life, the music of Bach or Beethoven is going to understandably sound foreign to you. I'd like to recommend music from various time periods for you to listen to and enjoy. Many of these titles can be found on YouTube or downloaded on the web. Or do it the old-fashioned way and buy a CD! Browse these and other musical pieces until you hear music that you enjoy and that fit the parameters for good music. Find enough to fill up your playlist with music that is godly. Now, some music will be obviously godly in music and in word, like good hymns. Some music is wordless, but by its order, rhythm, and timbre it imitates our God, who is a God of order and of beauty. Have fun perusing this list! It is divided into music of different time periods and styles. None of it is bad for your soul. You will like some pieces and dislike others. That's okay! You should also find plenty of good, edifying music that will minister to you. May God bless you with music that touches your soul and lifts your spirit to Him. I couldn't resist putting the ones I find particularly wonderful to listen to in **bold**.

MEDIEVAL

- Romanos the Melodist - "Nativity of Christ"
- Kassiani - "Igapisas Theophore"
- Guido of Arezzo - "Ut Queant Lapis"
- Hildegard of Bingen - *Voices of Angels*
- Bernart de Ventadorn - "Ben m'an Perdut"
- Gregorian chants were the songs sung by monks during the medieval period. They have a special quality and are important in the history of Western music. Listen to any of them!

RENAISSANCE

- Josquin des prez - *Motets and Chansons* - performed by Hilliard Ensemble
- William Byrd - *Consort Songs and Music for Viols* - performed by Gerard Lesne
- Guillaume Dufay - "Nuper Rosarium Flores"
- Claudio Monteverdi - *Madrigals*
- **Giovanni Gabrieli - *Canzonas and Sonatas***

- John Dunstable - "Agnus Dei" - this is like a later, harmonized Gregorian chant.
- Thomas Morley - *Various Madrigals and Canzonets* - performed by Ensemble Amarylis
- Andrea Gabrieli - "Ricercari"

BAROQUE

The two most important Baroque composers were Johann Sebastien Bach and George Friderich Handel, though there are many other rich composers in this era.

- **Johann Sebastian Bach** - arguably the best composer in history, he is certainly one of the most prolific. Really, anything by Bach is good, but some of his music seems to express his academia rather than his heart. Here's a list of some of my favourite Bach pieces.
  - "Sheep May Safely Graze"
  - "Jesu, Joy of Man's Desiring"
  - "Little Fugue (aka Fugue in G Minor)"
  - *St. Matthew's Passion*
  - *Brandenberg Concertos*
  - "Wachet Auf"
  - "Minuet in G from Anna Magdalena's Notebook"
  - *Ach Gott, wie manches Herzeleid*
  - "O Sacred Head, Now Wounded"
- Antonio Vivaldi
  - *The Four Seasons*
  - "Gloria in D"
  - "Credo RV 591"
- George Frideric Handel
  - *The Messiah*
  - *Judas Maccabaeus*
  - *Music for the Royal Fireworks*

- *Water Music Suite*
- *Serse*
- *Solomon* (especially "Arrival of the Queen of Sheba")
- "Zadok the Priest"
- Arcangelo Corelli
  - *Concerto Grosso in D Major*
- **Henry Purcell**
  - **"Trumpet Voluntary"**
- Georg Philipp Telemann
  - *Violin Sonata*
- Jean-Philippe Rameau
  - *First Concert in C Minor*
- **Johann Pachelbel**
  - **"Canon in D"**

CLASSICAL

Though most traditional music composed before 1900 is commonly called classical, and I have often used the term in this way throughout the book, there is actually one particular time period which is properly named Classical. Many of the great composers lived in this time period.

- Ludwig van Beethoven
  - **"Moonlight Sonata"**
  - **"Ode to Joy"**
  - **"Bagatelle in A Minor (Für Elise)"**
  - *Egmont Overture*
  - *Symphony #6*
- Wolfgang Amadeus Mozart
  - **"Horn Concerto #4"**
  - *Le Nozze Di Figaro*
  - **"Eine Kleine Nachtmusik"**

- *Piano Concerto #21*
- ***Symphony #40***
- Franz Joseph Haydn
  - *Trumpet Concerto in E*
  - *Farewell Symphony*
- Christoph Willibald Gluck
  - *Flute Concerto in G Major*
- Carl Phiipp Emmanuel Bach
  - *Cello Concerto in A Minor*
- Carl Stamitz
  - *Viola Concerto in D Major*
- Johann Christoph Bach
  - "Fürchte Dich Nicht"

ROMANTIC

- Chopin
  - "Minute Waltz"
  - "Ballade #1 in G Minor"
- Niccolò Paganini
  - "La Campanella"
- Franz Schubert
  - "Serenade"
  - ***German Mass*** (esp. "Sanctus")
  - "Moments Musicaux"
- Johann Strauss
  - "Wiegenlied"
  - "Emperor Waltz"
- Felix Mendelssohn
  - "O For the Wings of a Dove"
  - *Italian Symphony #4*

- Guiseppi Verdi
    - *Nabucco* (especially "Chorus of the Hebrew Slaves")
- Camille Saint-Saëns
    - *Le Carnaval Des Animaux*
- Pietre Illyich Tchaikovsky
    - *Piano Concerto #1*

TWENTIETH CENTURY

- Jean Sibelius
    - "Karelia Suite"
    - **"Finlandia"**
    - "Soluppgång"
- Debussy
    - "Claire de Lune"
- Gustav Holst
    - *Symphony in F, The Cotswolds*
- Benjamin Britten
    - *The Young Person's Guide to the Orchestra*

HYMNS

In the Hymns section I list several groups who perform hymns in an artistic and moral way. I can't guarantee that everything they produce is godly, but based on what I have heard from them, I feel safe in recommending them. Please use your own discretion and the leading of the Holy Spirit when choosing listening material in this and other categories.

- Oasis Chorale
- Classical Praise
- Adoration Ladies Ensemble
- Our Daily Bread - *Celtic Hymns*
- Anonymous Somebodies

- Fountainview Academy
- West Coast Baptist - "The Cause of Christ", etc.
- SMS Mens Chorus
- The King Family - *Journey of Hope*, etc.
- St. Michael's Singers

MODERN HYMNS

The Gettys have produced some really wonderful modern hymns. However, many of their performances of these songs include an unhealthy beat. Sing the songs; shun the recordings. Use a lot of discernment in the use of the music of Keith and Kristyn Getty and that of Stuart Townend.

MISCELLANEOUS CHRISTIAN

There's some crossover between this group and the previous one. These groups do mostly modern Christian music, but they also cover some hymns.

- The Garment of Praise
- **Emerald Chorale**
- Back to the Bible - in recent years they've been leaning to a more contemporary, rocky sound, but some of their earlier works are good.
- Galkin Evangelistic Team
- Hallal
- Hyles-Anderson College
- Keith Lancaster & the Acappella Company
- SE Samonte - This is a man who has collected the singing of various groups on his YouTube channel.
- Acapeldridge - This is one guy who sings various parts and records them together. Some of his music is great, some is too syncopated.
- Hylander Singing Men
- **The Hamilton Family**

BLUEGRASS

Jerusalem Ridge has several good bluegrass songs, and some that have a rocky beat.

- Dry River Boys - bluegrass
- **The Wissmann Family** (Go with songs by the family or the girls. Use more caution with the boys' music.)
- Nashville Bluegrass Ensemble

CLASSICAL GUITAR

- **Darren Curtis Skanson**
- Shirley Rumsey
- Heather De Rome
- Steven Novacek
- Jonathan Richards

MALE CHOIRS

- Holland Boys Choir
- Dunvant Male Choir
- Rhos Male Voice Choir
- The Blaenavon Male Voice Choir
- Voice of Praise

CHRISTMAS MUSIC

- *A Light Classical Christmas* - Darren Curtis Skanson
- *O Come, All Ye Faithful* - Joni Eareckson Tada et. al.
- *Christmas Carols for a Kid's Heart* - Joni Eareckson Tada & Bobbie Wolgemuth
- 16 Singing Men: *Carols of Christmas*
- ***Christmas Guitar* - Boccherini Guitar Quartet**
- *Christmas Concert* - Platinum String Orchestra
- *Best Loved Christmas Melodies* - Meta Epstein & Abel Mambreani

- *An Angel's Noel* - The Ware & Patterson Duo
- *Christmas Harp* - C.L. Del Mastro

MISCELLANEOUS

Groups in this category are recommended for their artistic merit in production of good music. They may perform pieces from a variety of genres.

- Jean Carignan - French Canadian, Irish and Scottish Fiddle Music
- Celtic Thunder - They're talented, but be choosy about which songs you listen to.
- **Chris Norman, the flute player**
- Alasdair Fraser and Natalie Haas - *Highlander's Farewell*
- Graham Townsend - *Classics of Irish, Scottish, and French-Canadian Fiddling*
- Hyles-Anderson College
- The Irish Tenors
- Morten Lauridsen
- The Macabeats - these guys can be really good or really bad in their musical styles - enjoy with caution.
- The Piano Guys are super talented and have some good music - and a lot of rocky music, too.
- John Powell - "See You Tomorrow" and others. He's a writer of music for films.
- Regimental Band of the Royal Hussars
- Simon Fraser University Pipe Band - *Affirmation* and *Live at*
- *Carnegie Hall*
- John Philip Sousa
- Pat Surface & The Boundary Water Boys - I have only heard "The Circle Game" from this group, but they show skill and talent that looks to be worth perusing.
- The von Trapp Children - *A Capella*
- Welsh Guards Band

Endnotes

CHAPTER 1

1. Don Stewart, "Is Ezekiel Speaking of Satan or the King of Tyre?" *Blue Letter Bible,* accessed May 22, 2019, https://www.blueletterbible.org/faq/don_stewart/don_stewart_82.cfm.

2. Maurice, *The Prophets and Kings of the Old Testament,* 28.

3. Gardiner, *Bach: Music in the Castle of Heaven,* 167.

4. Ibid, 17.

5. Shapiro, *Encyclopedia of Quotes About Music,* 233.

6. Cassiodorus, *Encyclopedia of Quotes About Music,* 182.

7. Spence-Jones, *The Pulpit Commentary, Volume 2.*

CHAPTER 2

1. Sacks, *Musicophilia,* 37.

2. Ibid, 40.

3. Levitin, *This is Your Brain on Music,* 7.

4. Kingsley, The Good News of God, Sermon XVII.

5. Smith & Carlson, *The Gift of Music,* 297.

CHAPTER 3

1. "Musical Notation," The Heart of Music 101, https://sites.google.com/site/theheartofmusic101/musical-notation, accessed April 10, 2020.

2. Levitin, *This is Your Brain on Music*, 220–221.

3. "In the Key of," Kala in Treble, https://kalaintreble.blogspot.com/2012/11/, accessed April 10, 2020.

4. Smith and Carlson, *The Gift of Music*, 294.

5. Abraham, *The New Oxford History of Music, Vol IV*, 419.

6. Hazlitt, *The Life of Luther Written by Himself*, 7.

CHAPTER 4

1. Wolff, *Bach, the Learned Musician*, 309.

2. paraphrased from, among other places, page 338 of *J.S.Bach: The Learned Musician*

3. Smith and Carlson, *The Gift of Music*, 298.

4. Ibid, 298.

5. Wolff, *Johann Sebastian Bach: The Learned Musician*, 337.

6. Hart, *Contemporary Christian Music Exposed*, 14.

7. Smith and Carlson, *The Gift of Music*, 271.

8. "Music Styles: Language of the Spirit Realm," Biblical Connection, accessed May 22, 2019, https://biblicalconnection.wordpress.com/2012/10/19/music-styles-communicating-in-the-spirit-realm

9. Peters and Peters, *Why Knock Rock?* 13.

10. Levitin, *This is Your Brain on Music*, 69.

11. Elvis Presley, "Hound Dog," 1956.

12. Benjamin Welton, "10 Concerts that Ended in Violence," accessed May 22, 2019, http://listverse.com/2015/12/01/10-concerts-that-ended-in-violence.

13. Smith and Carlson, *The Gift of Music*, 298.

CHAPTER 6

1. Wolff, *Johann Sebastian Bach*, 153.

2. Smith and Carlson, *The Gift of Music*, 205.

3. Eliot, "Gus, the Theatre Cat," *Old Possum's Book of Practical Cats*.

CHAPTER 7

1. Marshall K. Kirk and Erastes Pill, "The Overhauling of Straight America," *Guide Magazine*, 1987.

2. Ibid.

3. Plato, *The Republic*, (4.424c).

4. Dr. Robert B. Sloan, Jr., "But if Not," Presidential address at Houston Baptist University, February 18, 2009.

5. Dave Bohon, "Apollo 8 Astronaut Recalls Historic Scripture Reading From Space," *The New American,* December 24, 2013.

6. James J. S. Johnson, J.D., Th.D., "Genesis in Chinese Pictographs," *Acts and Facts,* February 27, 2015.

7. *Questions and Answers of World History,* (London: Arcturus Publishing Limited, 2008), 26.

8. Smith and Carlson, *The Gift of Music,* 298.

CHAPTER 8

1. John Newton, "Amazing Grace."

2. C. S. Lewis, *The Screwtape Letters, (*Samizdat Ebooks 2016), 50.

CHAPTER 9

1. Sacks, *Musicophilia,* 35.

2. Ibid, 100.

3. Ibid, 94–95.

4. Levitin, *This is Your Brain on Music,* 220–221.

5. Anita Nee, "A Child's Brain Develops Faster With Music Education," *Music Education Works,* June 19, 2016, https://musiceducationworks.wordpress.com/2016/06/19/a-childs-brain-develops-faster-with-exposure-to-music/ (Accessed January 16, 2020).

6. Levitin, *This is Your Brain on Music,* 190.

7. Tom Barnes, "Science Just Discovered Something Amazing About What Childhood Piano Lessons Did To You," January 8, 2015, https://mic.com/articles/108022/science-just-discovered-something-amazing-about-what-childhood-piano-lessons-did-to-you#.kGJhGlJH5, (Accessed January 16, 2020).

8. Don Robertson, "About Positive Music,Dove Song, 2010, http://www.dovesong.com/positive_music/plant_experiments.asp, (accessed February 10, 2020).

9. Monica Gagliano et. al., "Tuned in: Plant Roots use Sound to Locate Water," *Oecologica* 184, April 5, 2017, 151–160, https://link.springer.com/article/10.1007/s00442-017-3862-z (Accessed February 10, 2020).

10. Lorraine Eaton, "Mozart or Rock? For These Mice it was a No-Brainer," scholar.lib.edu, July 24, 1997, https://scholar.lib.vt.edu/VA-news/VA-Pilot/issues/1997/vp970724/07240420.htm, (Accessed February 10, 2020).

11. "Mice and Men," beet9hoven.blogspot.com, May 5, 2011, https://beet9hoven. blogspot.com/2011/05/mice-and-men.html. (Accessed February 10, 2020).

12. Marianna Wertz, "Why Classical Music is Key to Education," 1998, http:// www.schillerinstitute.org/programs/program_symp_2_7_98_tchor_.html (Accessed January 16, 2020).

13. Carol and Louis Torres, "Rhythm Rules," http://www.practicapoetica.com/ articles/rhythm-rules, (Accessed February 10, 2020).

14. Dennis Speed, "St. Thomas Choir Stuns Washington With Beauty of Music," *Executive Intelligence Review,* No. 8, 1998, 26–31, https://larouchepub.com/ eiw/public/1998/eirv25n08-19980220/eirv25n08-19980220.pdf (Accessed January 16, 2020).

15. Andrew Pudewa, "The Profound Influence of Music on Life," iew.com, https:// iew.com/sites/default/files/audiocourse/fileattachment/Effects_of_Music_ Life_Handout.pdf, (Accessed on February 10, 2020.)

16. Sacks, *Musicophilia,* 32.

17. Music Education Works, "Musical Training and Executive Functioning," 2016, https://musiceducationworks.wordpress.com/2016/03/21/musical-training-and-executive-functioning/ (Accessed January 16, 2020).

18. Levitin, *This is Your Brain on Music,* 185.

19. Ibid, 215.

20. Ibid, 9.

CHAPTER 10

The quotes from rock musicians were taken from David C. Cloud's book *Contemporary Christian Music Under the Spotlight,* 1998.

1. "Can Television Influence Your Child's Behaviour?" Novak Djokovic Foundation, https://novakdjokovicfoundation.org/can-television-influence-your-childs-behaviour.

2. "Iron Horse Nightclub has Conditions Places on Licence," *CBC News,* August 30, 2010, https://www.cbc.ca/news/canada/edmonton/iron-horse-nightclub-has-conditions-placed-on-licence-1.927931, (Accessed February 10, 2020.)

3. Pat Saperstein and Erin Nyren, "David Cassidy, 'Partridge Family' Star, Dies at 67," *Variety,* (2017), http://variety.com/2017/music/people-news/david-cassidy-dead-dies-partridge-family-1202618273 (Accessed January 16, 2020).

4. Pareles, Jon. "Have Rap Concerts Become Inextricably Linked to Violence?" The New York Times. The New York Times. Accessed September 2, 2020. http://www.nytimes.com/1988/09/13/arts/have-rap-concerts-become-inextricably-linked-to-violence.html.

5. Froeling, *Criminology Research Focus,* 301.

6. Benjamin Welton, "10 Concerts that Ended in Violence," (2015) https://listverse.com/2015/12/01/10-concerts-that-ended-in-violence/ (Accessed January 16, 2020).

7. Dan Frosch, "Colorado Police Link Rise in Violence to Music," The New York Times, September 3, 2007.

8. Graham Martin, F.R.A.N.Z.C.P, Michael Clarke, M.B., and Colby Pearce, B.A. (Hons), "Adolescent Suicide: Music Preference as an Indicator of Vulnerability," *Journal of the American Academy of Child and Adolescent Psychiatry*, Volume 32, Issue 3, (May 1993): 530–535.

9. Levitin, *This is Your Brain on Music*, 2 and 3.

10. Ibid, 252.

11. Alasdair Forsyth, Marina Barnard, and Neil McKeganey, "Musical Preference as an Indicator of Adolescent Drug Use," *Addiction*, Volume 92, Issue 10, (2006) http://onlinelibrary.wiley.com/doi/10.1111/j.1360-0443.1997.tb02850.x/abstract (Accessed January 16, 2020).

12. Jeffrey Arnett, "The Soundtrack of Recklessness: Musical Preferences and Reckless Behavior among Adolescents," *Journal of Adolescent Research*, Volume 7, Issue 3, (July 1992), 313–331.

13. Tom R.M. ter Bogt, Loes Keijsers and Wim H.J. Meeus, "Early Adolescent Music Preferences and Minor Delinquency," Pediatrics: Official Journal of the American Academy of Pedeiatrics, (2013) http://pediatrics.aappublications.org/content/131/2/e380 (Accessed January 16, 2020).

14. King, P. "Heavy Metal Music and Drug Abuse in Adolescents," *Postgraduate Medicine*, 83(5), (1988), 295–301.

15. This comment is not meant to condemn anyone on the basis of skin colour or place or origin. Those who bought and sold human beings were hugely at fault, and those who worshipped false gods were in the wrong in that regard. Both groups were engaging in wrongful acts, regardless of the colour of anyone's skin.

CHAPTER 11

1. Bruce K. Waltke and Cathi J. Fredricks, *Genesis: A Commentary* (Grand Rapids: Zondervan, 2001), 88.

2. Levitin, *This is Your Brain on Music*, 236–237.

CHAPTER 12

1. "Did the Wesleys Really Use Drinking Song Tunes for Their Hymns?" Practica Poetica RSS. Accessed September 2, 2020. http://www.practicapoetica.com/articles/did-the-wesleys-really-use-drinking-song-tunes-for-their-hymns.

2. Torrey Johnson, *The Evangel*, 1971.

3. Hart, *Contemporary Christian Music Exposed*, 14.

4. Hart, *Contemporary Christian Music Exposed*, 8.

5. MacArthur, *New Testament Commentary: Ephesians*, 260–261.

6. Warren, *The Purpose Driven Church*, 280–281.

7. MacArthur, *New Testament Commentary: Ephesians*, 257–258.

8. Pascal, Pensées, Vol. 33.

9. Wolff, *J.S. Bach*, 389.

CHAPTER 13

1. Francis A. Schaeffer, *How Should We Then Live?: The Rise and Decline of Western Thought and Culture* (Wheaton, IL: Crossway Books, 2005), 19.

2. Jeremiah Burroughs, *The Evil of Evils*, (Soli Deo Gloria Publications; Reprint Edition May 2, 2012), 2, 3.

CHAPTER 15

Alan Ives has written an excellent article entitled "The Difference Between Good and Bad Music". http://www.biblebelievers.com/Ives1.html

Bibliography

Gerald Abraham, ed., *The New Oxford History of Music, Vol IV, The Age of Humanism, 1540–1630*. London: Oxford University Press, 1954.

Johann Sebastian Bach and Pamela L. Poulin, *Precepts and Principles of Playing the Thorough-Bass or Accompanying in Four Parts*. Oxford: Clarendon Press, 1994.

Dave Bohon, "Apollo 8 Astronaut Recalls Historic Scripture Reading From Space," *The New American*, December 24, 2013.

Jeremiah Burroughs, *The Evil of Evils*, (Soli Deo Gloria Publications; Reprint Edition May 2, 2012)

Shu Ching, as quoted by Nat Shapiro in *An Encyclopedia of Quotes About Music*. New York: Doubleday, 1978.

David C. Cloud, *Contemporary Christian Music Under the Spotlight*. Washington: Way of Life Literature, 1998.

Eliot, T.S. "Gus, the Theatre Cat," *Old Possum's Book of Practical Cats,* (London, Faber and Faber, 1939).

Froeling, Karen T. *Criminology Research Focus*. New York: Nova Science Publishers, Inc., 2007.

Gardiner, John Eliot. *Bach: Music in the Castle of Heaven*. New York: Vintage Books, 2013.

Garlock, Frank & Kurt Woetzel. *Music in the Balance*. South Carolina: Majesty Music, 1992.

Goodall, Howard. *The Story of Music*. London: Chatto & Windus, 2013.

Grout, Donald Jay. *A History of Western Music*. New York: W.W. Norton & Company, 1980.

Hart, Lowell D. *Contemporary Christian Music Exposed*. USA: Hart Publishing House, 2015.

Hazlitt, William. *The Life of Luther Written by Himself*. London: H.G. Bohn, 1862.

"The Heart of Music," The Heart of Music 101, https://sites.google.com/site/theheartofmusic101/musical-notation, accessed March 30, 2020.

"In the Key of," Kala in Treble, https://kalaintreble.blogspot.com/2012/11/, accessed March 31, 2020.

Ives, Alan. *The Difference Between Good and Bad Music*. Washington: Way of Life Literature, 1993.

Johnson, James J. S., J.D., Th.D. "Genesis in Chinese Pictographs," *Acts and Facts*, February 27, 2015.

Kingsley, Charles. *The Good News of God: Sermons*. London: MacMillan & Co., 1880.

Kirk, Marshall K. and Erastes Pill, "The Overhauling of Straight America," *Guide Magazine*, 1987.

Lamont, Ann. *21 Great Scientists Who Believed the Bible*. Australia: Creation Science Foundation Ltd., 1995.

Levitin, Daniel J. *This is Your Brain on Music*. New York: Penguin, 2007.

Lucarini, Dan. *Why I Left the Contemporary Christian Music Movement*. New York: Evangelical Press USA, 2002.

MacArthur, John, Jr. *The MacArthur New Testament Commentary: Ephesians*, (Chicago, Moody Press, 1986).

Makujina, John. *Measuring the Music*. Pennsylvania: Old Paths Publications, 2002.

Marissen, Michael. "Johann Sebastian Bach Was More Religious Than You Might Think," *The New York Times*, March 30, 2018, accessed May 22, 2019, https://www.nytimes.com/2018/03/30/arts/music/bach-religion-music.html

Maurice, Frederick Denison. *The Prophets and Kings of the Old Testament: A Series of Sermons*. Cambridge: MacMillan and Co., 1853.

"Can Television Influence Your Child's Behaviour?" Novak Djokovic Foundation, https://novakdjokovicfoundation.org/can-television-influence-your-childs-behaviour/

Dan Peters and Steve Peters, *Why Knock Rock?* Bloomington: Bethany House Publishers, 1984.

Plato, *The Republic.*

Questions and Answers of World History, (London: Arcturus Publishing Limited, 2008), 26.

Oliver Sacks, *Musicophilia.* Toronto: Vintage Canada, 2008.

Francis A. Schaeffer, *How Should We Then Live?: The Rise and Decline of Western Thought and Culture* (Wheaton, IL: Crossway Books, 2005), 19.

Dr. Robert B. Sloan, Jr., "But if Not," Presidential address at Houston Baptist University, February 18, 2009.

Jane Stuart Smith and Betty Carlson, *The Gift of Music.* Wheaton: Crossway Books, 1980.

Smith, Kimberly. *Music and Morals.* Washington: WinePress Publishing, 2005.

Smith, Kimberly. *Oh, Be Careful Little Ears.* Washington: WinePress Publishing, 1997.

Henry D. M. Spence, *The Complete Pulpit Commentary: Volume 2.* Harrington: Delmarva Publications, 2013.

Tree of Life School. *Beautiful Music.* New Brunswick: Tree of Life School, 1997.

Bruce K. Waltke and Cathi J. Fredricks, *Genesis: A Commentary* (Grand Rapids: Zondervan, 2001)

Rick Warren, *The Purpose Driven Life,* (Grand Rapids, Zondervan, 1995).

Benjamin Welton, "10 Concerts that Ended in Violence," ListVerse, 2015, accessed May 22, 2019, http://listverse.com/2015/12/01/10-concerts-that-ended-in-violence/ .

Christoph Wolff, *Johann Sebastian Bach: The Learned Musician.* New York, London: W. W. Norton & Company, 2000.

Youth Who Have Found Freedom. *How to Conquer the Addiction of Rock Music.* Illinois: Institute in Basic Life Principles, 1993.

About the Author

Elizabeth King is a music teacher who has led choirs, bands, congregations, and a small orchestra. She is the music director at the ministry in which she works with her husband and children.

Elizabeth holds a Bachelor of Education with a Major in Music. She enjoys singing and plays classical guitar and euphonium, as well as dabbling in other instruments. Elizabeth has given countless music lessons on various instruments and has led instrumental groups and choirs from elementary to high school ages, as well as directing church choirs. She enjoys teaching music leadership to workers in her ministry and leading groups of children, youth, and adults in songs which bring the truth of God to their hearts. Elizabeth loves to make music, especially with her family.

www.ingramcontent.com/pod-product-compliance
Lightning Source LLC
LaVergne TN
LVHW041154080426
835511LV00006B/599